STANLEY

Basic
Tiling

PRO TIPS AND SIMPLE STEPS

Meredith® Books
Des Moines, Iowa

Stanley® Books
An imprint of Meredith® Books

Stanley Basic Tiling
Editor: Ken Sidey
Senior Associate Design Director: Tom Wegner
Assistant Editor: Harijs Priekulis
Copy Chief: Terri Fredrickson
Copy and Production Editor: Victoria Forlini
Editorial Operations Manager: Karen Schirm
Managers, Book Production: Pam Kvitne,
    Marjorie J. Schenkelberg
Technical Editors, The Stanley Works: Mike Maznio,
    Jim Olsen
Technical Proofreader: Pete Bird
Contributing Copy Editor: Jim Stepp
Contributing Proofreaders: Becky Danley, Raymond L. Kast,
    Debra Morris Smith
Indexer: Patsy Lyons
Electronic Production Coordinator: Paula Forest
Editorial and Design Assistants: Renee E. McAtee,
    Kathleen Stevens

**Additional Editorial Contributions from
    Art Rep Services**
Director and Producer: Chip Nadeau
Photo and Technical Art Direction: Dave Morse
Writer: Martin Miller
Design: LK Design
Photography: Inside Out Studios
Illustration: Dave Brandon, Mario Rossetti
Photo Purchaser: Nancy South
Construction Supervisor: Matt Wagner

Meredith® Books
Editor in Chief: James D. Blume
Design Director: Matt Strelecki
Managing Editor: Gregory H. Kayko
Executive Editor, Gardening and Home Improvement:
    Benjamin W. Allen
Executive Editor, Home Improvement: Larry Erickson

Director, Sales, Special Markets: Rita McMullen
Director, Sales, Premiums: Michael A. Peterson
Director, Sales, Retail: Tom Wierzbicki
Director, Book Marketing: Brad Elmitt
Director, Operations: George A. Susral
Director, Production: Douglas M. Johnston

Vice President and General Manager: Douglas J. Guendel

Meredith Publishing Group
President, Publishing Group: Stephen M. Lacy
Vice President-Publishing Director: Bob Mate

Meredith Corporation
Chairman and Chief Executive Officer: William T. Kerr

Chairman of the Executive Committee: E.T. Meredith III

Acknowledgments
Ceramic Tile Works
Westminster Ceramics
Provenza
Monocibec / Naxos
Stone Design Chicago
Laticrete
SunTouch
Dens-Shield
Durock
Aqua-Mix Sealers
Rubi Cutters
Delta
First Quality Supply
A-1 Minnetonka Rental
Emtek
Nob Hill Decorative Hardware Minnesota

Photographers
(Photographers credited may retain copyright © to the listed
    photographs.
L = Left, R = Right, C = Center, B = Bottom, T = Top
Ron Blakely: 8, 9 (TL), 11 (TL), 20 (B)
Robert Perron Photography: 7 (TL), 9 (TR), 10 (TL), 10 (TR),
    21 (TL), 21 (TC)
Kenneth Rice Photography: 7 (TR), 7 (BL), 7 (BR), 21 (TR)

All of us at Stanley® Books are dedicated to providing you with
the information and ideas you need to enhance your home and
garden. We welcome your comments and suggestions about
this book. Write to us at:
    Meredith Corporation
    Stanley Books
    1716 Locust St.
    Des Moines, IA 50309–3023

If you would like more information on other Stanley products,
call 1-800-STANLEY or visit us at: www.stanleyworks.com
Stanley® and the notched rectangle around the Stanley name
are registered trademarks of The Stanley Works and
subsidiaries.

If you would like to purchase any of our home improvement,
cooking, crafts, gardening, or home decorating and design
books, check wherever quality books are sold. Or visit us at:
meredithbooks.com

Note to the Readers: Due to differing conditions, tools,
and individual skills, Meredith Corporation assumes no
responsibility for any damages, injuries suffered, or losses
incurred as a result of following the information published
in this book. Before beginning any project, review the
instructions carefully, and if any doubts or questions remain,
consult local experts or authorities. Because codes and
regulations vary greatly, you always should check with
authorities to ensure that your project complies with all
applicable local codes and regulations. Always read and
observe all of the safety precautions provided by
manufacturers of any tools, equipment, or supplies,
and follow all accepted safety procedures.

CONTENTS

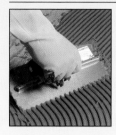

DESIGNING YOUR TILE PROJECT

Ceramic tile originates in materials of the earth, but those simple beginnings belie its versatility. No other material offers its array of color, shape, form, and texture, or brings so much excitement and variety to a design.

For centuries, ceramic tile has added durability and design to floors, walls, and other surfaces. Tile is so durable, in fact, that installations set 6,000 years ago look as fresh as if they were laid yesterday.

The versatility of tile doesn't stop there, however. You may think of it primarily as a traditional covering for kitchen floors and baths, but you can use it in any room of the house. It functions just as well in family rooms, dining rooms, bedrooms, and home offices. It's perfect for the hard use associated with children's play.

Installing tile is cost efficient, paying back its initial expense with reduced maintenance and replacement costs. In large floor installations, tile can add to the resale value of a home.

How to use this book

Your success with any tiling project will depend largely on how familiar you are with all of its aspects. Read through the entire book before starting your work. The first two chapters concentrate on design tips and methods for selecting materials. The next three chapters help you plan your project, carry out essential preparation tasks, and become familiar with basic installation techniques. After that, you're ready to apply your new knowledge to a floor, wall, or countertop.

Chapter 6 demonstrates techniques with photos and descriptions of each step.

What if . . .?

Since no two projects are alike, you may encounter conditions that depart from the norm. So if the steps shown for any task don't conform to your situation, check the lower half of the page for boxes that provide additional information. Those labeled "What if … ?" help you apply techniques to specific needs. You'll also find "Stanley Pro Tips," "Refresher Courses," and "Safety First" boxes. These items contain tricks of the trade, quick reviews of methods found elsewhere in the book, and information you need to keep in mind so that your work proceeds safely.

Tile can dramatically change the look of any room, and when properly installed, it will last a lifetime.

CHAPTER PREVIEW

Basic principles of design
page 6

Designing with color
page 8

Designing with scale, pattern, and texture
page 10

Start compiling a folder of information as you're planning your tiling project. Save clippings from home decorating magazines, brochures with photos of installations in designer homes, and color charts from home centers. All of this material will help you make informed design decisions.

BASIC PRINCIPLES OF DESIGN

In its simplest terms, design is a mood or look that is both visually appealing and physically comfortable. Design, however, does not start with aesthetics. It begins with decisions about how you want to use a room. After that, you employ a style that corresponds to that use.

For example, bedrooms are usually restful; dining rooms are comfortable and inviting; children's playrooms are colorful and active; and kitchens are functional and organized. No matter what surface you will be tiling, your choice of style should be consistent with your intended uses for that room. A family room, for example, may call for a boldly stated tile design. In a formal dining or living room, you may want the tiled surface to blend into the surroundings.

Definitions of style

Style can be categorized under two broad terms—formal and informal. Formal styles are characterized by symmetrical patterns, straight lines, right angles, and strictly geometric figures. Informal styles rely on curved lines, irregular edges, and random or asymmetrical patterns of decorative accents. A formal design conveys organization and order. An informal design is casual and free.

Within these broad categories are variations based on nationality, geography, and historical period. French, Art Deco, Southwestern, and contemporary are examples. Don't be overly concerned with terms or formulas—they may influence you to choose a style with which you might not feel comfortable.

Trust your intuition

Use your intuition as a guide when designing your tile project. Although modern trends in interior design, especially for floors, tend to favor muted or neutral colors, there's nothing that says you can't bend or break the rules to create a room with the right character and individuality.

Stick with your own ideas and incorporate the principles outlined in this chapter— color, form, pattern, texture, and scale— to achieve the look you want.

Formal tile installations, although characterized by regular geometric shapes and symmetrical arrangement of their elements, can still look lively and exciting. By carefully offsetting the tones of the wall tile with the sides of the tub surround, the homeowners have created an alternating pattern of light and dark vertical tile lines. The rectangular pattern is tastefully interrupted by the inset borders, complementing the classical look and creating a visual highlight that makes the room appear comfortable and stately at the same time.

STANLEY PRO TIP

How to choose a style that suits you

Discovering a style that best expresses your personality can be a confusing process. Here are some steps that will help you:
■ Read home decorating magazines and books. Gather photos of tile installations that appeal to you. Put your clippings in a folder.
■ When you visit friends' homes, pay close attention to locations where they have used tile. Make mental notes of colors and other decorative aspects—both things you like and those you don't like. Ask your friends about the advantages and disadvantages of the materials. When you get home, jot down your impressions and put your notes in the folder, too.

■ Visit tile suppliers, home furnishings stores, decorating showrooms, and home improvement outlets. File material samples, brochures, and paint chips in your folders.
■ When you're ready to plan your tiling project, go through your collection of design ideas. As you study them, you'll notice that certain themes emerge—colors, textures, and patterns that appeal to you. Make notes about these features and select those you think will look best on the surface you plan to tile.
■ Design the installation around these themes, modifying colors, patterns, and textures to suit the room and its uses.

Informal layouts, with curved outlines and irregular contours, can be difficult to design, but tile can prove especially helpful in solving such problems. In this shower area, the broken tile pattern and random colors create a contemporary Southwestern background in which the large showerhead is a perfect accent.

Period design doesn't have to slavishly follow a formula. This updated Arts-and-Crafts kitchen incorporates light slate-colored tile as a contrast to the period lighting and the simple but contemporary lines of the cabinetry. Notice how the orientation of the tile changes from countertop to the wall. Such subtle alterations and the thin linear accent on the wall help personalize the kitchen.

A country design scheme is a variation of an informal style that often combines warm and bright textures. Glazed terra-cotta floor tile and wide grout lines create a contrast that highlights the painted cabinets and refinished antique table. Area or throw rugs can make a tile floor feel warmer underfoot.

A contemporary design scheme will include many of the elements of a formal design style, as this kitchen demonstrates with its simplicity and straightforward, uncluttered lines. Contrasts are evident here, especially in the multicolored backsplash, which energizes the uniform natural finish on the cabinets.

DESIGNING WITH COLOR

Color is the most noticeable design element in a room; therefore it's the one that must be used with the most care. Review the photographs on these pages to see how the attributes of color work together to help create a particular mood. Keep these guidelines in mind to make your color selection easier.

■ Ignore color names. They can influence you more than you think. Take sample tiles of several colors home with you.

■ Trust your impulses—they indicate a preference for a certain color.

■ Samples will look different on the surface than in your hand. Set them on the floor or countertop or tape them to the wall.

■ Check colors at different times of the day and under different lighting. Sunlight will give the truest hue. Incandescent light adds a pinkish tone. Fluorescents may change the hue completely.

Experiment with color combinations, but remember that restraint is a good tool to use when mixing colors. Too much harmony can turn bland, and a combination that's too dynamic can be jarring.

Neutral colors or color schemes with low contrasts create a subtle background for other design elements in the room. In this eclectic blend of several styles, the light floor tile allows the furnishings to take center stage, highlighting the subtle differences in the tones of the curtains and the overstuffed chairs. At the same time, the floor complements the light tones in the rest of the room—the walls, lamps, comfortable couch, and coffee table. The whole interplay of similar colors and subtle contrasts opens up the room, adding to the spaciousness of the view through the divided picture window.

The vocabulary of color

HUE

Here are some terms you might hear in discussing the color of your tile with suppliers or decorators.

■ Hue is a pure color. Hue refers to a primary color by its name—red, blue, yellow.

■ Value defines the relative brightness of a hue. Colors of lower value (a murky red, for example) usually recede and make a room seem smaller.

WARM TONES

Those with high values (a bright green, for example) tend to stand out and can make a room appear airy and larger.

■ Tone describes whether the color is darkened (a shade) or lightened (a tint).

All of these aspects of color will work together to create a surface that either dominates your room or acts as a backdrop. A pattern with high

COOL TONES

contrasts (a checkerboard white on black tile, for example) will call attention to itself and not to the other elements in the room. Pastel tiles or tiles with earth tones will let other features of the room stand out.

Certain colors tend to evoke certain moods.

■ Reds and oranges create excitement; darker shades of both colors create warmth.

EARTH TONES

■ Yellows and whites are cheery—use them to brighten up a dark room. Too much of either, however, may be overpowering or sterile.

■ Greens and blues create calm; deep tones evoke associations with wealth, strength, and status.

■ Black is the universal contrast. It can make large rooms appear smaller.

Contrasts create interest. Tiling a surface with colors that contrast sharply, either within the tile pattern itself or with other colors in the room, will tend to call attention to the tiled surface. Here the blue glazed tiles and wide grout lines call attention to themselves, making the two-tiered countertop the focal point of the entire kitchen.

Borders can create contrasts in a design scheme, either with contrasting colors or with geometric patterns that accentuate or depart from the pattern of the field tile. Both elements come into play in this bathroom design. This black-and-white border both frames the large mirror and accents the square edges of the room.

Low, dense colors tend to make a room seem smaller. Although the predominant blue tones in this kitchen offer a cool contrast to the wood flooring and tiled wall, they also make the room seem dark, confined, and uninviting. When designing a room with little natural light, use low-value colors sparingly or not at all.

High, bright color values help make a room appear larger. Here the yellow wall tile and neutral white cabinets not only open up the appearance of the room, they also unify the pattern of tones and architecture of shapes in the room—the rectangular cabinets, the rounded island, and the triangular range hood.

DESIGNING WITH SCALE, PATTERN, AND TEXTURE

After you have chosen the color scheme for your tiling project, turn your attention to the size of the tile (its scale relative to the room size), the pattern in which you will set it, and the textures. All will affect the atmosphere you create.

Scale your project to the size of the surface so the tiles will seem balanced. Tile size and pattern can dramatically alter the appearance of a room.

Choose patterns consistent with your style and textures that will enhance it. The rough, uneven surface of handmade pavers, for example, can impart a rustic feel to a Southwestern or colonial design. For a more formal effect, set machine-made pavers with a smooth surface and precise edges. Use glazed tiles on your countertop and walls to brighten up the area. Vary the texture within wall designs with embossed floral accent tiles interspersed in the field. Or cap the layout behind a formal cabinet with engraved border tiles.

Squares create a formal appearance, but that doesn't mean your design has to be stiff. The lemon-tree insert on the back wall of this range hood breaks up the uniformity of the glazed wall tile with color and texture. Do-it-yourself accent patterns like this are available in kits.

Patterns can define the mood of a room as effectively as color. Like color, they require careful application. To avoid being overly repetitive, alternate rows with tole of a slightly varied pattern and tone. Patterns can soften hard corners and make decorating nooks and crannies easier.

ALTER THE APPEARANCE OF A ROOM
The effect of scale and pattern

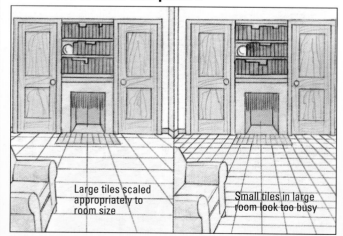

Large tiles scaled appropriately to room size

Small tiles in large room look too busy

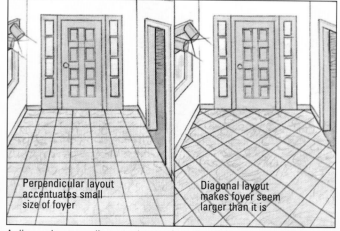

Perpendicular layout accentuates small size of foyer

Diagonal layout makes foyer seem larger than it is

Both scale and pattern can have dramatic effects on the perceived size of the room and on its ambience. Large tiles tend to call attention to themselves and can make a room look smaller. They look best in large rooms. Small tiles tend to get lost in a large room. They look more appropriate in a small area.

A diagonal pattern distracts the eye from the perimeter of the room and can work wonders in making a small area seem larger than it is. Small patterns can add an air of informality. Large formal and informal patterns can function as decorative accents.

Texture can make a room feel relaxed. The rough textures of this floor tile are complemented by the rough herringbone pattern and enhanced by careful placement of different color tones. The rough textures soak up light, enhancing the informal mood of this family room and home office.

Glazes present a smooth texture that brightens up a room, regardless of the color of the tile. Rectangular wall tiles set in a horizontal running bond pattern lend elegance to this bathroom. The period feeling is enhanced by the embossed border tile capped off with a curved trim.

Slate makes an excellent floor for all rooms, especially entryways. Its neutral surface acts as a background for any design scheme and its naturally rough surface provides a built-in nonslip safety feature. Slate is also durable. Hard slates are easy to maintain; softer Indian slates require sealer.

SAFETY FIRST
Texture and safety

Texture contributes to the design of your tiled surface and is an important safety feature as well.

Make sure that tiles laid on bathroom and kitchen floors—areas that are likely to get wet and slippery—have a nonslip surface to reduce the risk of falling. Avoid high-gloss glazed tile in these areas. If glazed tile is necessary, select one whose surface contains carbide chips or is otherwise designated as a nonslip tile. For stair treads, install a tile with a built-in tread.

Help with design
Don't be afraid to ask questions. Many home centers retain professional designers on staff.

STANLEY PRO TIP: **Evenly spaced tiles save money**

Save money on your tile project by installing tile whose dimensions fit as evenly as possible on the surface you are designing. An evenly spaced layout means less cut tiles, less waste, and less installation time. Measure the room and divide both its length and width by the combined width of the tile and grout joint. A slightly larger or smaller pattern that still meets your design requirements may be a better choice than a tile size that requires many cut edges. Changing the width of the grout joint can affect how the tile fits in the room.

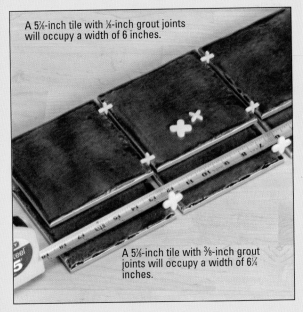

A 5⅞-inch tile with ⅛-inch grout joints will occupy a width of 6 inches.

A 5⅞-inch tile with ⅜-inch grout joints will occupy a width of 6¼ inches.

CHOOSING THE RIGHT MATERIALS

The more you know about the various kinds of tile, the easier it will be for you to design and install a practical and durable layout.

In this chapter, you'll find information about the different kinds of tile carried by suppliers, the various forms in which tile is manufactured, and what kind of tile works best in different settings.

You'll learn about membranes, mortars, and mastics, which, along with substrates, provide the foundation for the tile. After reading the chapter, you'll know which products will best suit your tile installation.

How to shop for tile

When you first begin to explore tile selections in your area, you don't need to start with a specific list of materials. In fact, after you make some general decisions about the way you want the room to look, it's probably better to take a look at the selection offered by several suppliers. That way you'll be able to compare prices from one outlet to another, and you may encounter materials you had not even thought of. Take samples home, fit them to a trial layout, and if they don't work, go back to the store and choose some other samples.

Make a list of the physical characteristics of the tile you need. Ask plenty of questions and choose a supplier who wants your business. Don't buy from a supplier who cannot provide you with manufacturer's specifications about permeability, durability, and maintenance. Look for an outlet that will lend or rent tools. A store that offers seminars and workshops will likely provide good service support after a sale. Additionally, look for a supplier who is willing to review your plans.

Once you have settled on a style and material, make sure that trim tiles are available for the project also. It's usually impossible to match trim tile from one manufacturer with field tiles from another. An alternative is to use wood, metal, or PVC trim materials, available in a variety of finishes and colors.

Purchase all the tiles and materials you need from the same supplier. That way you will be assured that everything is compatible.

Tile terms

The terminology used to describe tiles and materials may vary among suppliers and from region to region.

Porcelain tile, for example, may mean large modern floor tile to one supplier and small hexagonal mosaics to another. What one dealer calls an "isolation" membrane may be a "slip sheet" to another. Clarify things as you go, so you know what you're buying. Many tile sizes are listed as nominal, not actual. The actual size of a 6×6 tile, for example, may be 5⅞×5⅞ inches to allow for the width of the grout joint.

A little study and planning provide all the know-how you need to select tile for any project.

CHAPTER PREVIEW

Types of tile
page 14

Tile formats
page 16

Trim tile, borders, and edgings
page 18

What kind of tile to use
page 20

Selecting materials for a new tiling installation can be an adventure. Visit as many general and specialty stores as time permits. This will give you a broad base of information and may provide you with additional options and ideas for your projects.

Substrates and setting beds
page 22

Membranes and adhesives
page 24

Grouts, caulks, and sealers
page 26

STANLEY PRO TIP

Check local building codes

Communities establish building codes to ensure that materials and construction are safe and meet minimum quality standards. Although most tiling projects are not likely to require building permits, check with your local building department officials to make sure your installation is not subject to local codes.

TYPES OF TILE

Tile falls into categories based on the type of materials and methods used in its manufacture. Variations in either the material or manufacturing process affect not only how the tile looks, but also its quality, use, and cost.

Ceramic tile

The term ceramic refers to any hard-bodied material made from clay and hardened by firing at high temperatures.

Although a few specialty tiles are made from clay only, most modern ceramic tiles contain a mixture of refined clay, ground shale or gypsum, and other ingredients that reduce the shrinkage of the tile as it's fired.

Once mixed with water, the clay bisque gets its shape by being squeezed into a mold, pressed into a die, or cut like cookies from sheets. From there, temperatures from 900°F to 2,500°F harden the bisque. Most ceramic tiles are fired at about 2,000°F. In general, higher temperatures produce a denser tile. Most tile goes through the firing process only once, but some are fired twice. Others with decorative glazes are fired up to five times. The more firings, the higher the cost.

Nonceramic tile

Some nonceramic tile originates from clay mixtures, but it is fired at lower temperatures than ceramic varieties. Others composed of unrefined clay and bonding agents don't get fired at all, but dry naturally or in low-temperature kilns. Handmade tiles, such as saltillo, have a resulting rough texture and absorb water readily. They need to be sealed, but their natural imperfections can add rustic charm to a room. Cement-bodied tiles are made from a mortar and sand mix and are cured by chemical reaction.

Natural stone tile

Natural stone—marble, granite, slate, travertine, and others—is cut from quarry deposits and sliced into thin sections for installation. You'll find natural stone finished in a variety of textures, from coarse to highly polished. Its retail cost reflects the expense of its manufacture.

Quarry tile, extruded and fired at high temperatures, is semivitreous or vitreous. Made in ½- to ¾-inch thicknesses, it is fired unglazed with bisques in many colors, sizes, and shapes—4- to12-inch squares and hexagons, and 3×6-inch or 4×8-inch rectangles.

Porcelain tile, made of highly refined clay and fired at extremely high temperatures, absorbs virtually no moisture. Most porcelain tiles are unglazed, but glazed varieties are available. Sizes range from 1×1-inch mosaics to large 24×24-inch pieces, some with stone-look patterns.

Choosing tile for different locations

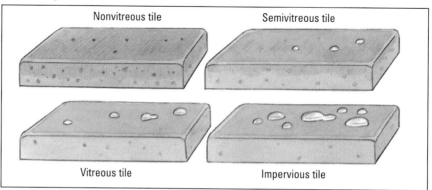

Nonvitreous tile   Semivitreous tile

Vitreous tile   Impervious tile

Tile varies in its ability to absorb water, and its vitreosity should be a factor in choosing tile for different locations.

Nonvitreous tile can absorb more than 7 percent of its weight in water and is not suitable for areas that will get wet.

Semivitreous tile has an absorption rate of 3 to 7 percent—good for family rooms but not for outdoor use.

Vitreous tile is dense, absorbs only 0.5 to 3 percent of its weight in water. You can install it in almost any location.

Impervious tile is almost completely water-resistant. It is more commonly found in hospitals, restaurants, and other commercial installations than in residential settings.

Terra-cotta tile, though technically not a ceramic because it is fired at low temperatures, is a low-density, nonvitreous tile suitable for dry areas. Its surface defects add to its charm. Available sealed or unsealed, it comes in squares from 3 to 12 inches and in other geometric shapes.

Cement-bodied tile is mixed from sand and mortar and is cured, not fired. The result is a nonvitreous tile with excellent durability. Although many have a rough-hewn texture, some colorful varieties are made with polymer designs. Available in squares or rectangles from about 6 to 9 inches.

Dimensioned stone, usually marble, granite, or slate, is cut from natural stone and tumbled, honed, or polished. Tumbled stone has a rough texture. Honing creates a matte-finish surface, less slick than polishing. Available in sizes ranging up to 12 to 24 inches square.

Tile technical terms

As you make decisions about tile purchases, you may encounter the following terms associated with tile manufacturing:

Bisque: The clay body of the tile. Bisque that is "green" has not yet been fired.

Cured: Describes bisque dried naturally or in low-temperature kilns

Extruded: A process in which wet clay is squeezed under pressure into a mold

Fired: Bisque hardened in high temperatures

Glaze: A hard, thin layer of pigment applied to the tile to give it color and protection

Vitreosity: The resistance of a tile to water absorption, ranging from nonvitreous (very absorbent) to impervious (almost completely water-resistant)

Glazes

Glazes made of lead silicates and pigments brushed or sprayed onto the surface of the tile add both color and protection. Some glazes are applied to the bisque before it's fired. Others go on after the first firing and are fired again. Single-fired tiles exhibit greater strength and durability. Additives introduced to the glaze will provide the surface of the tile with a texture.

Glazed tiles are water-resistant, but the grout joints between them are not. Even when grouting tiles with a latex- or polymer-modified grout *(page 26),* you should seal the joints.

Unglazed tiles soak up water and always need sealing to prevent water from penetrating them and damaging the adhesive or surface below.

TILE FORMATS

In addition to differences in materials and methods of manufacture, tile comes in many formats. The format of the tile can affect both where you choose to use it and the method with which you install it. Tile formats fall into two broad categories: loose tiles and sheet-mounted tiles, with different subcategories of each.

Loose tiles

Much of the tile you are likely to lay will be loose tile; that is, each piece requires that you set it individually and space it consistently to keep it straight. The term loose tile has broad applications. Every type of tile comes in loose formats, but some have limited application. Most loose tiles can be set in both organic mastic or thinset mortar, but some can be applied only with thinset mortar *(page 25)*.

Sheet-mounted tiles

Sheet-mounted tiles come prespaced and mounted on various kinds of backings. Sheets translate into reduced time and effort required to properly space small tiles. Sheet-mounted tiles are usually vitreous and almost always smaller than 4 inches.

Face-mounted tiles are held together with a removable sheet of paper that remains in place until you set the sheet of tiles and the mortar cures. Moistening the paper allows for easy removal.

Back-mounted tiles are joined with paper or a plastic mesh that stays in place when you set the tile.

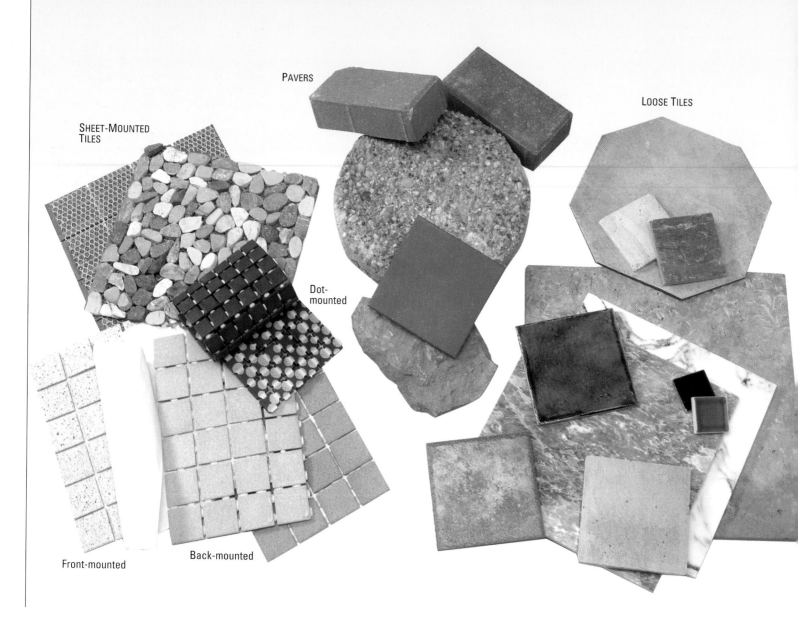

PAVERS

LOOSE TILES

SHEET-MOUNTED TILES

Dot-mounted

Front-mounted

Back-mounted

Dot-mounted tiles are fastened to each other with plastic or rubber dots on the sides of the tile. The dots remain in place when the tile is installed.

All mounting materials cut easily with a utility knife, but they display a potential for weakening the bond of the adhesive. Most sheet-mounted tiles should be set in thinset mortar *(page 25).*

Mosaic tile

Any tile less than 2 inches wide is in the mosaic category. Once set by hand and now almost always sheet-mounted, mosaics are made as porcelain, clay, or glass tiles. They range from 3⁄32 to 1⁄4 inch thick, with the individual tiles manufactured in 1⁄4- to 2-inch squares, rectangles, or hexagons. Glass tile mosaics are usually limited to 1-inch squares. Mosaics are sold in a wide range of colors and patterns. Most are unglazed, but glazed varieties are available.

Pavers

The term *pavers* defines a category of loose clay, shale, or porcelain tile at least 1⁄2-inch

thick and designed primarily for floors. Certain types will also make a suitable wall or countertop surface.

Machine-made pavers are generally fired as semivitreous or vitreous tile, both glazed and unglazed, in 4×6-inch and up to 12-inch squares. Vitreous pavers work well on walls and countertops.

Handmade pavers, both glazed and unglazed, are nonvitreous. Some are as much as 2 inches thick; most come in 4- to 24-inch squares. You can set handmade pavers on walls, but their porosity prohibits use in shower enclosures and on countertops. Both machine-made and handmade pavers should be set in thinset mortar. Rough-textured tile requires additional mortar on the back (a process called back-buttering) so it will adhere more securely *(page 81).* All unglazed tiles should be sealed.

Brick-veneer tile

Brick-veneer tile is manufactured with several different methods. Some are real brick cut in thin cross sections. Other

coarsely textured varieties are made from clays similar to those used in tile production, but they are fired at low temperatures. Still others are actually a cement-bodied tile.

You can set brick veneer in both outdoor and indoor locations, whether they are wet or dry. Brick veneer in shower walls and tub surrounds, however, will prove almost impossible to clean, and the low durability of imitation brick generally limits its use to wall installations. Brick veneer can be set in either organic mastic or thinset, the latter required for outdoor use.

Glazed wall tile

Although many floor tiles can be used successfully on walls, glazed wall tiles—usually nonvitreous with a soft glaze—are made specifically for walls.

Wall tiles are usually 1⁄4-inch thick and fired in 4 1⁄4- and 6-inch squares; larger sizes are also available. When installed with a waterproofing membrane, they are suitable for wet locations, such as shower and tub surrounds. They can be set in either organic mastic or thinset *(page 25).*

What's on the back?

On the back of most pieces of tile you'll find various configurations such as raised ridges, dots or squares. Some of the configurations, dots or buttons, for example, are built into the tile to allow them to be stacked so heat in the kiln will pass evenly over all surfaces.

Regardless of the manufacturer's purpose, all patterns increase the rear surface area of the tile. The more surface with which the adhesive comes into contact, the stronger the adhesive bond. Ridges on a tile can actually increase its surface area up to three times.

Some tiles are engraved or embossed with information that records a specific run of tile, manufacturing process, or location. These marks can help you match tiles in historic restoration or remodeling.

Spacers and lugs

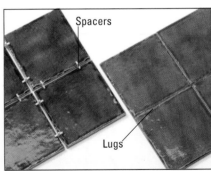

Spacers

Lugs

Many tiles, most commonly those made for walls, have lugs molded into their edges to help you space them accurately. Nonlugged tiles require separate spacers.

Small plastic spacers are made in various shapes and sizes and in 1⁄16- to 1⁄2-inch widths. You may find rectangular spacers better than X-shaped spacers for holding wall tiles firmly in place.

TRIM TILE, BORDERS, AND EDGINGS

Trim tiles finish your installation and hide the edges of the field tiles. Borders and edgings have a similar function, but their contrasting shapes, colors, designs, and patterns add accents to your layout.

Buying trim tiles

As you plan your layout, visualize or sketch the trim tiles you will need. Buy them from the same manufacturer so the color and finish match. Be sure to price the trim—trim tiles can cost twice as much as similar size field tiles. If you can't find trim to match, consider wood, metal, or PVC edgings.

Buying borders and accents

Borders are usually used to define edges or as accents among field tiles. When you plan the pattern of your layout, be sure to include these tiles so you will have a good idea of its final appearance.

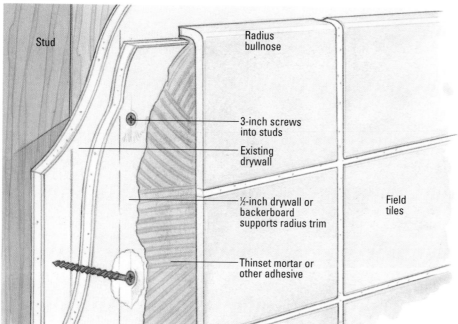

Trim tiles come in a variety of configurations to satisfy the design requirements of almost any installation. Edge trim has one or two rounded edges for use along the perimeter of walls and countertops. You can also install it as base tile for a floor. Wall trim is similar—use it where you want a full-size tile and don't need a special edge treatment. Some trim tiles are made especially for countertops. Quarter-round and out corners provide a smooth and stylish transition between the countertop surface and the front edges.

RADIUS TRIM

Radius trim is made so its rounded lip actually turns a right-angled corner at the edge of the tile. In installations in which the setting bed is raised over the existing wall surface, the turned edge covers the thickness of the setting bed. Use it on the perimeters where you have installed backerboard over drywall.

Install a wood edge

Install a wood-trim edge if you cannot find V-caps or bullnose tiles to finish out your countertop.

Because wood expands at a different rate than tile and adhesive, separate it from the tile with a bead of caulk. Use a caulk that matches the color and consistency (sanded or unsanded) of the grout.

You can fasten the wood edge to the countertop with finishing nails, or screws and plugs *(page 107)*.

V-capped edging allows you to finish off almost any tile installation with professional looking results. The lower leg of the cap takes the place of a separate cut tile to face the front edge of the countertop base. Both legs of the cap require back-buttering with adhesive *(page 107).*

Base tiles finish off a floor installation, and most made specifically for this purpose have a coved foot at their base. Bullnose floor tiles are sometimes available. If base tiles are not available in the same style as your field tile, you may be able to cut field tile and use it as trim.

Borders and accent tiles can spice up any installation. A border tile is usually a narrow length that is used to finish off an edge. Accent tiles, some made of glass, can take almost any form, but usually have a contrasting color, size, shape, or texture.

Types of thresholds

Tiled floors are generally higher than the adjacent floors, and thresholds bridge the floors to make the transitions easy, safe, and attractive.

■ Flush thresholds lie between the two floor surfaces and are used when there is no height difference. The edges of both floors need to be parallel to ensure their proper installation.

■ Metal thresholds are the easiest to install and come in a variety of types. Z-bar is a form of metal threshold used where tiled floor meets carpet.

■ Hardwood thresholds are beveled on two planes and fastened to the lower wood subfloor with finishing nails or screws.

■ Stone or synthetic materials also provide safe and attractive transitions. Ask your supplier for suggestions that will match your installation.

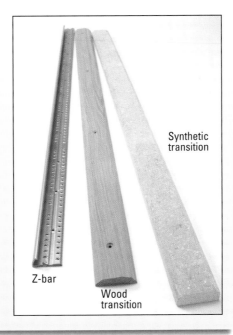

Synthetic transition

Z-bar

Wood transition

STANLEY PRO TIP

Rounding the edges

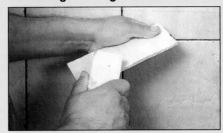

Some manufacturers do not make trim tile in the same style or colors as their field tile. If the tile is a soft-bodied variety, you may be able to fashion trim tile yourself by rounding the edges with a masonry stone.

Making your own trim demands accuracy and effort. Pull the stone toward you, keeping the pressure even and the angle consistent on the edge of the tile. Make frequent comparisons to tiles you have already shaped.

WHAT KIND OF TILE TO USE

When it comes to choosing tiles for a particular room or setting, there is perhaps only one unbending rule— you can use many floor tiles on walls and countertops, but you can almost never set wall tiles on such horizontal surfaces. Your choice needs to account for durability, maintenance requirements, and safety. Many manufacturers will specify how their tile can be used.

Floor tiles

Floor tiles are generally ⅜- to ¾-inch thick (although pavers are thicker). In general, porcelain, quarry, and terra-cotta tile, both glazed and unglazed, and cement-bodied tiles are suitable for floors. However, even within these categories, tile quality varies. Check the tile's rating to make sure it will stand up to the requirements of your room. Terra-cotta floor tile, for example, is not as durable as porcelain, so you might not want to use it in an entryway. Choose glazed tiles that are slip-resistant. Seal soft-bodied tile against moisture and stains.

Wall tiles

Most wall tile is made from a white-bodied clay (floor tiles are generally red-bodied) in thicknesses not much more than ¼ inch. Their thin profile keeps them light enough to be supported on wall structures. Since they are not subject to the abuse of floor tiles, in most rooms color and style will be your main considerations. In shower enclosures and tub surrounds, however, choose a vitreous wall tile that will not absorb water. Avoid porous tile such as brick veneer, even dense varieties. Porous tile attracts bacteria and will be impossible to clean. If using a heavy floor tile, make sure the structure and setting materials are strong enough to support it.

On the countertop

You'll want vitreous or impervious tile on your countertop, preferably glazed for easy cleanup. Scratch a sample with a kitchen knife to make sure the glaze will stand up to countertop use.

Family rooms receive constant use and heavy traffic but their atmosphere is informal. Choose a high-quality, dense floor tile such as this large porcelain tile that can take the abuse and not show wear. Irregular shaped tiles add a touch of informality.

Countertops take a beating from chopping, mixing, dropped utensils, spills, and frequent cleanup. Some vitreous floor tiles, such as this porcelain marble look-alike, make excellent countertops. So do stone and glazed tile, if the glaze is impervious. Hard, dense tiles make cleanup easy.

Choosing the right tile

Foyers and entryways receive heavy use in all kinds of weather. Foot traffic brings in moisture and grit that will quickly wear away a soft tile surface. Take durability and maintenance into consideration when choosing entryway tile. Hard, vitreous tile should be included among your choices, and any glazed tile should come with a nonslip surface.

Foyers and entryways are good places to make a style statement. They are the first element in a home that visitors or friends see and contribute to that important first impression. They are well suited to formal designs. To enhance a formal tiled entryway, consider a geometric mosaic border or an arrangement that features angular elements in pairs.

Wall tile doesn't have to stand up to the wear and tear that floor tile does, so it will play a decorative role in most rooms. Let design guide your choices and use borders to vary the pattern. Pregrouted tile panels install easily and require less maintenance than grouted tile.

Kitchen floors: Tile is a traditional choice for kitchen floors because it cleans easily. Choose vitreous tile and seal the grout. Throw rugs will soften the floors hard surface underfoot, and in-floor radiant heating or an electric heat mesh will warm it in colder climates.

Bathrooms: Sheet-mounted ceramic mosaics, which are vitreous and highly resistant to water, make excellent bathroom surfaces. On walls that won't get wet you can use standard wall tile with a soft glaze. For floors, shower enclosures, and tub surrounds, use a vitreous tile.

Tile wear ratings

Manufacturing associations grade ceramic and stone tile according to its wearability.
Ceramic tile grades:
■ Group 1: Tile suitable for walls only
■ Group 2: Suitable for residential floor use, but not in heavy traffic areas, such as kitchens or entries
■ Group 3: Suitable for all residential areas
■ Group 4 and 5: Tiles suitable for commercial applications
Dimensioned stone grading:
■ Group A: Uniform and consistent; not subject to breakage
■ Group B: Similar to Group A, but more subject to breakage and surface damage
■ Group C: Natural variations may increase risk of breakage
■ Group D: Often the most beautiful, but the most subject to damage and repair

STANLEY PRO TIP: **Matching outdoor tile to the climate**

Tiling an outside patio will provide you with a durable and easy-to-maintain surface that's ideal for relaxation and for entertaining family and friends.

Since patios are subject to outdoor weather conditions, choose tile that will withstand the climate in your area. Porous, nonvitreous tile will absorb moisture and may be fine for warm, dry climates, but it will likely crack in cold, freezing weather.

Patio tile needs a concrete slab as a base. If you don't already have a slab, that requires excavation and pouring concrete. With the slab in place, your tiling will proceed as it would indoors. Use a mortar mix that will withstand the outdoor elements.

Patio tile often continues from outdoors to inside on the entryway floor. Make sure your selection meets the needs of both installations.

SUBSTRATES AND SETTING BEDS

Tile requires a surface that is stable and flat. You can tile over properly prepared concrete, drywall, and plaster, but other surfaces call for a substrate (see chart on *page 39*). Plywood, even exterior grade varieties, is not suitable. Its high absorbancy pulls water out of the mortar, and its faster expansion rate increases the potential that cracks will occur.

Drywall
Drywall, a core of gypsum compressed between two layers of heavy paper, provides an appropriate substrate for wall installations that won't get wet. Drywall is not suitable in wet areas. It is manufactured in different size sheets (4×8 feet is standard) and thicknesses (½ inch is common on walls). In wet areas, remove existing drywall to the studs and install a waterproofed backerboard or a waterproofing membrane and cement backerboard.

Greenboard
Greenboard is a drywall product whose paper layers are treated for water resistance. It is available in different thicknesses, but ½ inch and ⅝ inch are used on walls. You can install it in locations that will receive infrequent moisture, but it won't stand up to repeated wetting. In any wet location, it's better to use backerboard.

Cement backerboard
Cement backerboard is a cement-based material formed in one of two methods. A cement core is sandwiched between layers of fiberglass mesh or the fibers are impregnated in the core. Cement board is the most prevalent substrate for both wet and dry installations. It is made in 32- or 36-inch widths and in lengths up to 60 inches, in ¼- and ½-inch thicknesses.

Another backerboard made of cement, ground sand, cellulose fiber, and additives does not contain fiberglass mesh. It is lighter than cement board, cuts easily, and includes an imprint to guide fastener placement. It comes in 4×8 sheets and ¼-and ½-inch thicknesses.

Glass-mat gypsum backerboard
Not to be confused with gypsum drywall, this material is constructed of a compressed gypsum core with embedded fiberglass and a vinyl-like water-resistant coating. It is lighter and easier to cut than cement board but not as strong. It is available in 4×8 sheets and ¼- and ½-inch thicknesses.

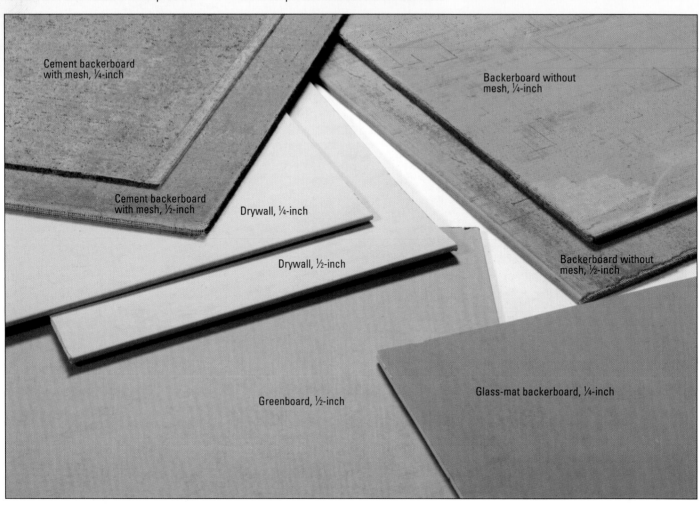

Cement backerboard with mesh, ¼-inch

Backerboard without mesh, ¼-inch

Cement backerboard with mesh, ½-inch

Drywall, ¼-inch

Drywall, ½-inch

Backerboard without mesh, ½-inch

Greenboard, ½-inch

Glass-mat backerboard, ¼-inch

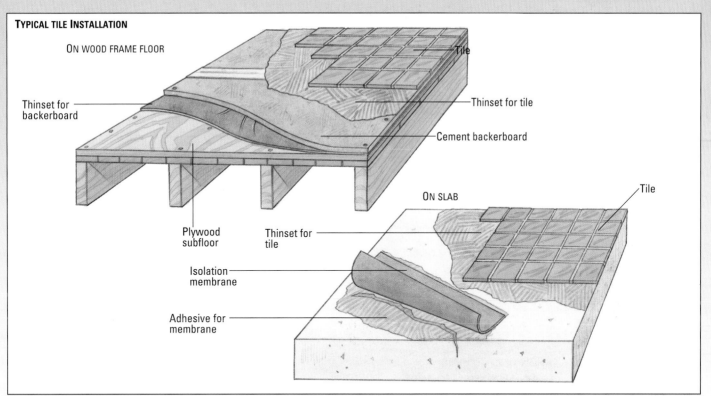

TYPICAL TILE INSTALLATION

ON WOOD FRAME FLOOR

Tile

Thinset for backerboard

Thinset for tile

Cement backerboard

Plywood subfloor

ON SLAB

Tile

Thinset for tile

Isolation membrane

Adhesive for membrane

In a typical tile installation, the plywood subfloor provides a stable foundation and supports the weight of the tile. Cement backerboard laid on the subfloor in a bed of thinset mortar is screwed to the plywood and joists. Tile is set in a mortarbed and grouted. Slab installations may require an isolation membrane to keep cracks from telegraphing to the tile. Wet locations, such as shower enclosures, need a waterproof membrane under the backerboard.

Self-leveling compounds

Self-leveling compounds, technically not a substrate, are used to level depressions in slabs and subfloors. Most call for only light mixing with water and level themselves when poured. Quick-setting brands allow tiling within hours.

Self-leveling compounds work best when applied in thicknesses of less than 1 inch. If using a compound in a deeper depression, make more than one pour, but check the manufacturer's directions first.

Pour the compound after completing all other repair work. Leaving the application until last ensures that the compound stays clean and ready for tiling.

Don't substitute drywall screws

Screws made for backerboard installation are treated with a corrosion-resistant coating and are formed with self-countersinking heads. Drywall screws are not a good substitute—their heads may snap off and moisture may cause them to rust.

Purchase 1¼-inch fasteners when installing backerboard directly to studs and 2-inch screws when fastening backerboard over ½-inch drywall.

MEMBRANES

Wherever an installation exhibits a danger of cracking the tile or allowing water to penetrate into the subsurface, you need to install a membrane.

Isolation membranes
These materials allow cracks or different materials to expand and contract without telegraphing the movement to the substrate and tile.

Two-part membranes, adhesive and mesh or chlorinated polyethylene (CPE), are applied directly to the surface to be tiled. The easiest materials to use employ a roller-applied adhesive. On old, stable concrete, you can cover each crack separately. On new concrete and floors that you suspect will develop cracks with age, apply the membrane to the entire floor.

Waterproofing membranes
Use a waterproofing membrane in shower enclosures and other areas that will get wet. Felt paper, polyurethane sheets, and two-part membranes can be used as waterproofing membranes. Many products function as both a waterproofing and isolation membrane.

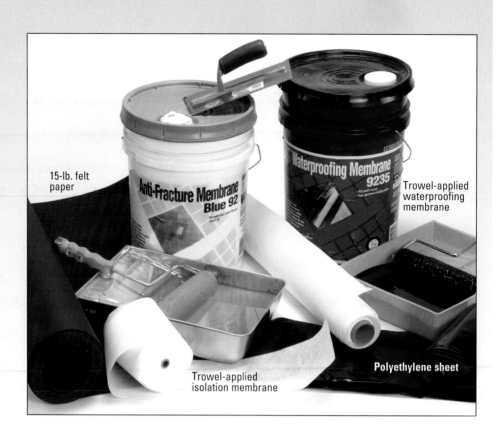

15-lb. felt paper

Trowel-applied waterproofing membrane

Trowel-applied isolation membrane

Polyethylene sheet

STANLEY PRO TIP: **When to use isolation membrane**

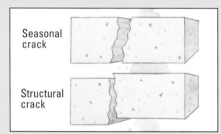

Seasonal crack

Structural crack

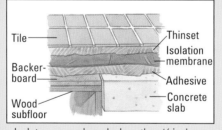

Tile — Thinset
— Isolation membrane
Backer-board —
— Adhesive
Wood subfloor — Concrete slab

Look closely at a slab floor and you may discover that it contains two different types of cracks.

Seasonal cracking occurs when temperature changes cause the material to expand. At a seasonal crack, the concrete moves laterally, leaving the separated surfaces of the material at the same height.

Structural cracks, caused by vertical shifts in the slab, leave one edge of the crack at a different height than the other.

Isolate seasonal cracks less than ⅛-inch wide with a membrane to prevent them from being transmitted to the tile surface. Isolation membranes will not keep structural cracks out of your tile surface, however. Fix the cause of a structural crack before setting the tile.

Because different materials expand at different rates, tile applied continuously over slab and wood floors may crack where the two floors join. Use an isolation membrane at these junctures *(page 59)*.

Sound-control membranes
Modern home building methods have reduced the size of the structural members without sacrificing their strength. While these practices reduce costs, they also result in thinner walls that transmit sound more easily from room to room.

If your planned tile project contains a wall or floor that separates a noisy area from a quiet one—for example, a family room over or next to an office—ask your supplier about a sound-control membrane.

Sound-control membranes come in different forms and are applied in the same fashion as membranes used for waterproofing and crack isolation. Some products are multipurpose.

ADHESIVES

Adhesives hold the tile in place and can generally be divided into three categories.

Thinset mortar

Thinset mortar is the most commonly used adhesive in tile installations. It is almost always the best product for floors and has wide applications in wall tiling installations. It offers great flexibility in placing tiles when wet, and when cured it provides greater strength than organic mastic.

Epoxy thinset

Epoxy thinset sets up quickly. Its hard, impermeable consistency makes it useful in settings requiring chemical resistance. This thinset is expensive and hard to apply; in most cases, it's best installed by the pros.

Organic mastic

Organic mastic is made with either a latex or a petroleum base and a carrier that evaporates and leaves a bonding agent stuck to the tile. This adhesive is not as strong or flexible as thinset. It is, however, good for flat walls in prime condition. Make sure it's compatible with your materials.

Dry-mixed thinset mortar

Organic mastic

Epoxy thinset

Premixed thinset mortar

THINSET MORTAR
Additives and mixing

Although not impervious to water, thinset exhibits highly water-resistant properties. Thinset mixed with water, however, may crack when cured. To improve its flexibility, mix it with a latex additive, following the manufacturer's directions. This also improves the bond strength of the thinset, which is essential with vitreous or impervious tile such as porcelain.

Thinset comes in premixed thinset or mix-it-yourself varieties—a choice that comes down to preference and cost.

Premixed brands cost more, but mixing your own offers several benefits. You can adjust the mixture to a wide range of weather conditions, making it wetter in hot and dry climates or stiffer in cold and humid conditions. You can also alter its consistency to provide optimal adhesion over a wide range of substrates and tiles.

Working with mastic

Stir the mastic if necessary, but do not thin it. If it has begun to harden, do not use it. Apply only enough to an area you can set within its "open" time (the time it takes the product to skim over). Clean tools and tile immediately with the proper solvent.

SAFETY FIRST
Handling adhesives

Thinset and other adhesives contain caustic ingredients. Solvent-based adhesives are potentially explosive and harmful when inhaled. Wear gloves and a respirator when mixing all adhesives and keep the area well ventilated.

GROUTS, CAULKS, AND SEALERS

Grouts, caulks, and sealers complete a tile installation.

Grouts

Grout fills the joints between tiles, but it does more than simply take up space. Grout strengthens the overall tile surface, adds flexibility and reduces the tendency of the tiles to crack, helps prevent water damage to the subsurface, and contributes to the design of the installation.

You can buy grout premixed or you can mix your own. Premix offers increased convenience but is slightly weaker. If the powdered grout you purchase does not contain a dry polymer, mix it with a latex additive instead of water for increased flexibility, strength, color retention, and mildew and stain resistance. Sanded and unsanded grouts come in colors to match any tile.

Caulks

Caulks are flexible materials used instead of grouts in joints that require maximum flexibility—expansion joints, around sinks and plumbing fixtures, and inside tiled corners.

Buy caulk in tubes for use with a caulk gun or in squeezable tubes. It comes in both sanded and unsanded mixtures and in many colors. Always use silicone caulk. Latex caulk is not as durable and changes color over time.

Sealers

Sealers prevent liquid and stains from penetrating tiles and joints.

Penetrating sealers work their way into the surface of the material. Topical sealers remain on the surface of the tile in a thin layer and depending on the product can alter the appearance of the surface *(page 112)*.

To seal joints, use an applicator designed specifically for this purpose. Use a mop or sealer applicator to seal the surface of unglazed tiles.

Sizing the joints

Certain kinds of tile generally look best with grout joints of a specific width.
- Glazed tiles: 3/16 to 3/8 inch.
- Porcelain tiles: 1/8 to 1/4 inch.
- Terra-cotta tiles: 3/4 inch.
- Cement-bodied tiles: 3/8 to 1/2 inch.
- Granite, marble stone tiles: 1/16 inch.
- Slate tiles: 3/8 to 1/2 inch.

Use these dimensions as a guide. You can vary the size to suit the aesthetics of your installation and to make tiles fit evenly across the room, but larger joints are more likely to crack. Irregular tiles such as saltillo and other handmade pavers usually need large joints to make their edges look even and aligned with one another.

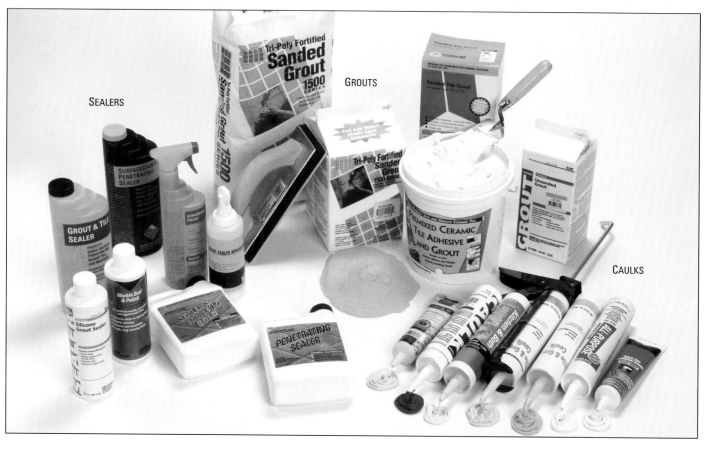

SEALERS

GROUTS

CAULKS

What type of grout to use

Type	Description and Uses
Unsanded grout	Portland cement and additives. Used for grout joints of 1/16 inch or less in ceramic tile, marble, granite, and other stone installations.
Sanded grout	Portland cement, sand (for strength), and additives. Used for grout joints wider than 1/16 inch. As the joint width increases, use grout with larger sand particles.
Epoxy grout	Epoxy resins and hardeners. Used for high chemical and stain resistance and in installations exposed to high temperatures. Also used with epoxy thinset to grout mosaics.
Colored grout	Unsanded or sanded grout with color additives. Premixed packages in hundreds of colors. Colors that contrast with the tile emphasize the geometry of the pattern. Grouts similar to the color of the tile will de-emphasize the pattern.
Mortar	Portland cement, sand, and additives mixed in proportions suitable for masonry installations, to set brick pavers, slate, or rough stone.

Don't forget to use expansion joints

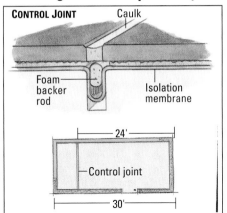

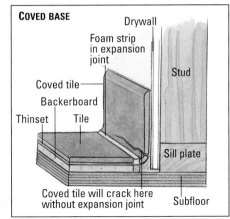

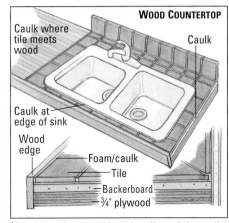

When tile or a masonry surface covers a large expanse or where any of those materials meet a different material, their expansion will subject them to cracking. These locations require a cushion—an expansion joint.

Expansion joints are filled with a foam backer rod and topped off with caulk. Include the foam strip on your shopping list if you're tiling any of the surfaces or situations shown above.

Control joints (above left) are separations in sections of a concrete slab. They are built in on the perimeter and every 24 feet within slab when it's poured. Tile laid on a concrete slab will need an expansion joint over these points. Without the foam backer rod, the movement of the slab will be telegraphed to the tile, causing it to crack *(page 91)*.

Allow for an expansion joint also at the perimeter of tiled floors (above center). Leave a 1/4-inch gap between the edge tile and the wall or the base of a coved tile base. Fill this gap with foam backer rod and cover it with caulk colored the same as your grout.

Countertop tiles move, too, so allow for an expansion joint where the countertop tiles meet the backsplash (above right).

Fill the gaps with backer rod to the base of the tile and caulk the tile joint with colored caulk.

PLANNING YOUR TILE INSTALLATION

Nothing contributes more to the success of your tiling project than careful planning. Planning helps you produce attractive, professional-looking results, and it organizes the job. A well-drawn, detailed layout plan will help you create a more accurate cost estimate than sketches or generalized notes.

One aspect of remodeling, however, can't be solved with graph paper and a ruler—the disruption and mess. To minimize the stress, anticipate debris disposal. Collect sturdy cartons for hauling out old flooring, drywall, or plaster. Order your materials early and get all the preparation out of the way by the delivery date. If you won't be done by the time the materials arrive, plan where to store them—away from the project site. Have all the right tools before you begin the job. Nothing stalls a project—or your enthusiasm—more than running back and forth to the hardware store.

If the kitchen will be shut down, make alternate arrangements for meals. Coordinate the removal of bathroom fixtures with your family's daily schedule.

Use this list to keep your tiling project organized from start to finish:
■ Measure all rooms carefully and calculate their areas.
■ Create a scaled drawing and layout plan of the surface you'll be tiling.
■ Estimate material quantities, starting with underlayment and other preparation materials: adhesives, grouts, and fasteners. Be sure to include the trim tile.
■ Make a list of the tools you'll need. Purchase or rent them. Plan your work so you can return rented tools within 24 hours to minimize costs.
■ Estimate your total costs, including any for alternate living arrangements if needed. When shopping for tile, visit several suppliers to get the best deal.
■ Plan for temporary storage of furniture and other objects. Store furniture in little-used rooms to keep disruptions in your life to a minimum.
■ Prepare a construction calendar to keep yourself on schedule.

Careful planning is the key to every successful tile installation.

CHAPTER PREVIEW

Making a layout drawing
page 30

A dimensional floor plan
page 32

A dimensional wall plan
page 34

Measure tile samples to transfer accurate tile pattern to scaled drawing.

Arrange planning materials on large flat work surface with all materials at hand.

Scaled drawing on graph paper helps iron out design and layout problems in advance.

STANLEY PRO TIP

Principles of layout

When you are experimenting with various layouts on paper, these few guidelines will help you design an attractive installation:

■ Use as many full tiles and as few cut tiles as possible.

■ Cut tiles should not be less than one-half of a tile.

■ Balance the edges of the installation so that the cut tiles are the same width on opposite walls.

■ If you have to taper the tiles on an edge, place them away from visual centers, along a far wall, or behind furniture.

MAKING A DIMENSIONAL LAYOUT DRAWING

A dimensional layout drawing puts all the details of the surface you'll be tiling on paper. It reflects not only the outline of tiled surfaces, but also the layout of the tile.

A dimensional layout drawing can help you plan precisely, assist a supplier in helping you make estimates, and act as the basis for answering other questions about your project.

Making a drawing proceeds in a fairly straightforward manner. The process begins with a rough sketch on which you post the measurements of the room. Next, make a scaled drawing based on the sketch and measurements. In the final stage, use tracing paper to draw in the tile pattern or to experiment with options.

Although tile is sold in cartons whose contents cover a specified number of square feet, counting the tiles on your layout drawing will give you a more accurate estimate, especially if your project contains several cut tiles.

PRESTART CHECKLIST

☐ **TIME**
About an hour to sketch and measure a medium-size kitchen. Time for making a dimensional layout plan will vary with the complexity of the design and the number of alternative layouts drawn.

☐ **TOOLS**
Sharp pencils, measuring tape, ruler, architect's scale, plastic drawing square

☐ **SKILLS**
Measuring and drawing accurately

☐ **PREP**
Selection of tile

☐ **MATERIALS**
Large sheets of graph paper and tracing paper, masking or drafting tape

Before you measure the room, make a rough sketch of its contours. Start in a corner and measure to the nearest ⅛-inch the length of every surface where it changes direction. Post the measurements on the sketch as you go. A floor sketch should note the dimensions of appliance recesses, cabinets, and built-in furnishings. A sketch of a wall or countertop should account for anything on the surface that interrupts a line of tile, such as windows or electrical outlets.

TYPICAL DIMENSIONAL DRAWING

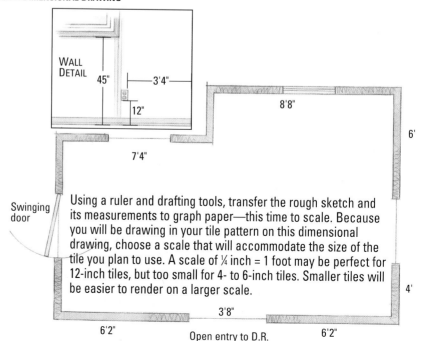

WALL DETAIL

45"

3'4"

12"

8'8"

6'

7'4"

Swinging door

Using a ruler and drafting tools, transfer the rough sketch and its measurements to graph paper—this time to scale. Because you will be drawing in your tile pattern on this dimensional drawing, choose a scale that will accommodate the size of the tile you plan to use. A scale of ¼ inch = 1 foot may be perfect for 12-inch tiles, but too small for 4- to 6-inch tiles. Smaller tiles will be easier to render on a larger scale.

4'

3'8"

6'2"

Open entry to D.R.

6'2"

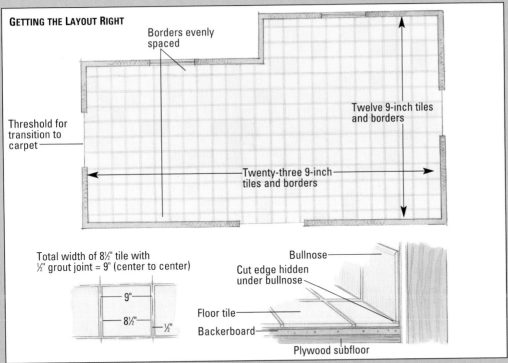

GETTING THE LAYOUT RIGHT

Borders evenly spaced

Threshold for transition to carpet

Twelve 9-inch tiles and borders

Twenty-three 9-inch tiles and borders

Total width of 8½" tile with ½" grout joint = 9" (center to center)

9"

8½"

½"

Bullnose

Cut edge hidden under bullnose

Floor tile

Backerboard

Plywood subfloor

Tape your dimensional drawing securely to your work surface; then tape a piece of tracing paper over it. Carefully draw your tile layout on the tracing paper. Experiment with various designs, using new sheets of tracing paper until you arrive at the layout that looks best in the room. Use the total of the tile width plus the width of the grout joint in determining the layout. The edges of cut tiles can be hidden under toekicks, along an inconspicuous wall, or under a countertop backsplash. If possible, doorways should start with a full tile and edges should end in at least a half-tile border.

Estimating materials

To estimate the materials needed, first compute the area of the surface by multiplying its length by its width. For complicated surfaces, compute the overall area and subtract the space in the nooks and crannies.

Estimate tile quantities by dividing the coverage-per-carton into the total area and adding 10 percent for breakage, cut tiles, and mistakes. Count the tiles on your layout drawing for a more precise estimate. Save unused tile for future repairs.

Figure backerboard quantities by dividing the sheet area into the surface area. Grout and adhesive coverage will vary among manufacturers. Consult your supplier for assistance. Don't forget tape, screws, and other materials.

HALF-TILE BORDER
Revise the layout

If your first layout doesn't result in evenly spaced half-tile borders, try adjusting the grout lines. If things don't come out evenly, revise your layout. Remove the partial tiles and the full tiles on each axis. Redraw the layout with the remaining section of full tiles centered in the room. This will leave enough space for wider tiles at the borders. Measure to the edge and divide it by 2. In this example seventeen 2-inch border tiles and fifteen 12-inch full tiles were removed, leaving a space of 14 inches ÷ 2 = 7 inches, or more than a half-tile at each border.

This method also allows you to make more accurate material estimates. If you count the tiles in the first layout, you'll find there are 55 full tiles and 17 cut tiles. Counting the tiles in the final layout results in an estimate of 40 full and 32 cut tiles.

Preliminary layout with uneven borders

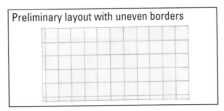

Layout with tiles removed

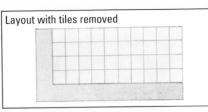

Final layout with more than ½-tile borders

Laying out irregular tiles

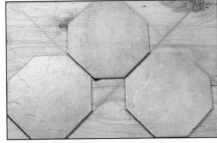

Almost all irregularly shaped tiles have a reference point you can rely on when making your dimensioned layout. Use a ruler to lightly draw in layout lines and space them to conform to the tile-grout dimension. Cut a thin cardboard template scaled to the overall configuration of a square of the tile and use the template to draw trial layouts.

Most irregular tiles are sold by the square foot. To make material estimates, divide the total area by the coverage per carton.

TIPS FOR MAKING A DIMENSIONAL FLOOR PLAN

One of the most common problems in planning a floor installation is out-of-square walls. Walls seldom define a room squarely, but you can make paper-and-pencil adjustments much more easily than rebuilding a wall.

To determine if the area is square, use the 3-4-5 triangle method (illustrated below). Snap a chalkline on the floor, or tack a mason's line at the midpoints of each pair of opposite walls. From the intersection, measure out on one line a distance of 3 feet. Tape the line at that point and measure and tape a distance of 4 feet on the other line. Now measure the distance between the tapes. If it's 5 feet exactly, the floor is square. Adjust the lines, if necessary, until they are perpendicular. Now measure from the lines to the out-of-square walls at each end and post this measurement on your drawing.

Wavy walls may also affect your drawing. Check them with a 4-foot level and represent the condition on your drawing as accurately you can.

Check the floor to determine if it is level and flat. If the floor is out-of-level it won't affect the final look unless you are also tiling a wall. But floors must be reasonably flat (within an ⅛-inch in 10 feet) to keep the tile from cracking. For more on leveling floors, see *pages 56–59*.

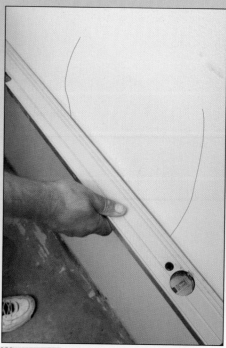

Wavy walls will affect the contour of the edge tiles on floors. Use a 4-foot level to check the lower surface of the wall near the floor. Minor variations in the surface can be remedied in a number of ways.

CHECKING FOR SQUARE WITH 3-4-5 TRIANGLE METHOD

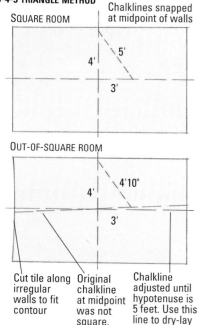

SQUARE ROOM — Chalklines snapped at midpoint of walls — 5' — 4' — 3'

OUT-OF-SQUARE ROOM — 4'10" — 4' — 3'

Cut tile along irregular walls to fit contour — Original chalkline at midpoint was not square. — Chalkline adjusted until hypotenuse is 5 feet. Use this line to dry-lay tile.

WHAT IF ...
The floor is not square?

Hide tapered cuts under baseboard, behind furniture, or on inconspicuous wall.

Diagonal layout distracts the eye and makes taper less noticeable.

An out-of-square floor surface will result in tapered tiles on at least one edge. Draw the tiles on your layout plan to minimize the visibility of the tapered tiles. Modify the grout width, hide cut edges under toekicks, or arrange your layout so the tapered edges fall behind furniture (left). Try a diagonal layout (right) or a larger, irregular tile to hide the tapered edges. In extreme cases, you can shim out the wall and rebuild it.

Laying out different configurations

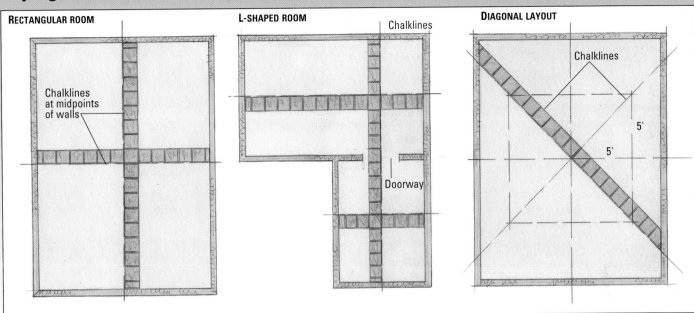

RECTANGULAR ROOM

Chalklines at midpoints of walls

L-SHAPED ROOM

Chalklines

Doorway

DIAGONAL LAYOUT

Chalklines

5'

5'

In a rectangular or square room, pencil in reference lines at the midpoints of the walls and draw in tiles on both axes. If you have the tiles, lay them out on the floor to make your drawing more accurate. Adjust the placement of the lines so the pattern ends in even borders, if possible.

When laying out an L-shape room, position the lines so they carry from one room to the other. Adjust them so the layout results in even borders if necessary.

To establish lines for a diagonal layout, first pencil in lines at the midpoints of the room. Then on each axis, mark an equal distance from the intersection. Extend these points until the extensions intersect. Draw diagonal lines from the intersections through the midpoint.

WAVY WALLS
Hide or fix the problem

Wavy walls can result in edge tiles on the floor with uneven cuts. If the problem is not severe, the cuts may not be noticeable.

When drawing a layout plan, try the following solutions. Minor variations in a wall surface may actually "disappear" if hidden under a baseboard.

More severe depressions in a wall can be leveled with a skim coat of thinset prior to tiling the floor *(page 63)*. Feather the edges of the skim coat to blend in with the level surface. Skim coating, however, requires proper preparation of the wall so the mortar will stick *(page 39)*. You will also have to tile the wall or paint it, or cover it with another material.

STANLEY PRO TIP

What to do in doorways

When you are preparing a dimensioned layout plan, draw the tiles in so a full tile will fall with its edge in the center of a doorway. If you can't set a full tile in the doorway because your plan already incorporates wide border tiles, you may be able to minimize the effect of a cut tile with a threshold in the doorway *(page 96)*.

If the tile continues into an adjoining room, center a tile at the doorway, if possible, so that an even portion falls in each room.

WHAT IF . . .
The floor is not level?

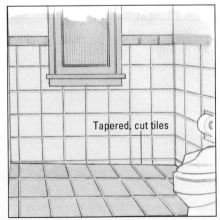

Tapered, cut tiles

An out-of-level floor creates tapered wall tiles at the floor. A diagonal wall layout may fix a minor condition, but not as well as on a floor. For severe problems, install a wall covering other than tile.

TIPS FOR MAKING A DIMENSIONAL WALL PLAN

Walls can exhibit the same out-of-square conditions as floors. Walls might also be out of plumb (their surface may not run true to vertical) and their surfaces might be wavy. You need to perform some routine checks and identify any problems on your layout drawing.

Any of these conditions on one wall may not be noticeable if it is not too severe and if you are not tiling an adjacent wall or the floor. These problems do become more noticeable, however, when tiling a neighboring surface.

Use a 4-foot level to check the walls, as shown on this page. Note or show on your plan how the condition will affect your layout. Adjust the pattern of the tiles as necessary to deal with the problem. For example, measure the amount by which the edge of the wall is not square and draw the edge on your layout plan to reflect its angle. Draw cut tiles on this line. Making the tiles as wide as possible will improve the appearance of the edge.

Check for plumb: Before drawing in the pattern of your wall tile, check the wall to see if it is plumb. Hold a 4-foot level vertically at the corner of the wall. If the spirit bubble centers in the glass, the wall is plumb. Repeat the process on the adjacent wall if you are tiling it also. An out-of-plumb wall will not be as distracting if you are not tiling the neighboring wall.

Out-of-plumb wall

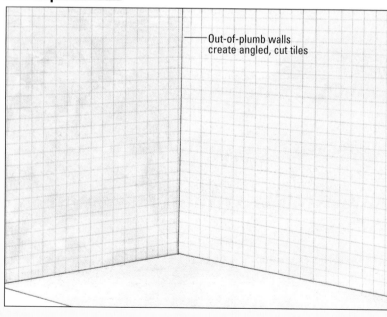

Out-of-plumb walls create angled, cut tiles

If your plans call for tiling adjacent walls and if one or both of them is not plumb, now is the time—when the plans are still on paper—to consider possible solutions.

For minor discrepancies, apply a skim coat of thinset mortar *(page 63)* at the corner of the out-of-plumb wall, bringing the mortar out on the surface far enough that when you sight down the wall, it appears plumb to the other one. Check your work with a 4-foot level.

You can also plumb the wall by nailing or screwing vertical shims to the wall from floor to ceiling. Then screw backerboard to the wall and tape it *(page 74)*.

If the condition is extreme, you can remove the wall surface to the framing and recover it with backerboard or drywall, shimming it out on the studs. Don't tile adjacent walls that are out of plumb.

Uneven surface: Like floors, walls must be reasonably flat. Wall tiles on an irregular wall surface are not as likely to crack as floor tiles, but an uneven surface is much more noticeable on a wall than a floor.

HIDING OUT-OF-SQUARE WALLS

Rigidly uniform tiles accentuate tapered cuts   Rough, irregular tiles diminish effect of tapered cuts

Walls that are out-of-square will require that you cut tapered tiles in the corners. If the condition is not severe, you may be able to make it less noticeable by arranging your layout so that you have at least one-half to three-fourths of a tile at the edges. Slightly adjusting the grout width across the entire surface of the wall may help you space the edge tiles more evenly. Rigidly uniform tile will accentuate tapered cuts. Consider using a larger irregular tile and/or an accent pattern to diminish the effect of tapered cuts. Set the cut tiles in the back corner of side walls where they will be less noticeable.

WHAT IF ...
Walls are not flat?

Wavy walls will not be very noticeable when tiled if the variations in the surface are broad and not severe.

Correct minor depressions by skim coating them to level with thinset *(page 63)*. Feather the edges of the skim coat. Check your results by sighting down the surface of the wall with a 4-foot level.

For severe problems you may need to resurface the wall with backerboard, shimming it to level.

STANLEY PRO TIP: **Walls with windows**

How you lay out a wall with a window depends somewhat on the width of the wall. On long walls with a centered window, pencil a line through its midpoint and draw in an evenly spaced tile pattern on either side of it. If the window is not centered, draw a line midway between the edges of the window and the corners.

Walls shorter than 8 feet will show uneven edges more dramatically. Try to position a full tile at the window with even cut tiles at the edges *(page 98)*. Bullnose tile at the window may also help even out the placement.

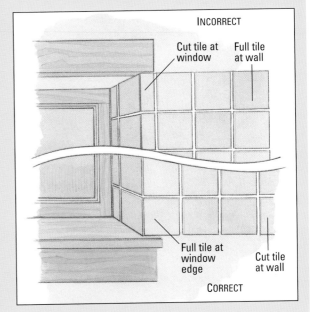

PREPARING SURFACES FOR TILING

Preparing a floor, wall, or countertop for tiling may account for more than half of the work associated with your project. Careful preparation pays off—the installation will go more quickly and the results will look better. Different surfaces require different preparation steps. The chart on *page 39* provides a quick overview of the necessary steps.

Structural requirements
If you are tiling a surface in new construction, you can ensure the surface meets the requirements for tile as the structure is being built. If you're renovating an existing room, you may have to take steps to retrofit the surfaces, making them sound, plumb, flat, and level. Existing surfaces are rarely perfect and almost always need work, but correcting them generally requires only basic tools and skills and a small dose of patience.

Tile adds substantial weight to a floor. This chapter shows some methods to strengthen floor structures. Other floors may require more extensive work better left to a professional contractor. Consult an architect or contractor if in doubt.

Organize your work
Plan the work in sections. When possible, do the easier tasks first and work your way up to more difficult chores. Most projects begin with removing something, ranging from trim or moldings to major appliances. The topics in this chapter are presented in the general order in which they should occur. Read through the chapter in its entirety and then make a list of the tasks that apply to your installation.

Take your time and work carefully. Undoing mistakes can make the job more difficult and expensive.

Tools and materials
For each project, make a list of the tools and materials you need and bring all of them to the work area before starting. Nothing will slow you down more than repeated trips to the basement, garage, or hardware store.

Tile requires strong and stable surfaces. Proper preparation is essential and saves time and money.

CHAPTER PREVIEW

General room preparation
page 38

Removing molding and baseboards
page 40

Removing appliances
page 42

Removing fixtures
page 44

Small sledge hammer used for heavy mortar work

A cold chisel is hardened steel for cutting tile and grout.

Repairing or removing the existing floor
page 50

Preparing a wood subfloor
page 56

Preparing a slab floor
page 58

Preparing walls for tile
page 60

Removing countertops
page 66

Installing a new countertop base
page 68

GENERAL ROOM PREPARATION

Before you begin any demolition or preparation, take steps to keep dust and debris localized to the room in which you're working.

Protect the surfaces
If you're not tiling the floor, protect it with a tarp or heavy-duty drop cloth. Tape the drop cloth if necessary to keep it from moving and exposing the existing floor as you work. Heavy rosin paper is an option, but mesh reinforced plastic tarps are inexpensive and reusable.

Lay tarps on hallways outside the work area to keep floors from being scratched by tracked-in dust. A small rug (a carpet sample works well) placed just outside the door of the work area will remove debris from your shoes.

Remove any furniture and protect built-in cabinets, bookshelves, and other fixtures with old bed sheets. Cabinets and vanities generally don't require removal unless the subfloor needs repairing.

Clear the air
Keep dust from migrating into other rooms.

Tape cardboard over heat and return-air ducts (remove the floor registers if tiling the floor). Tape plastic sheets over open entries or tack up an old bed sheet to allow access to another room. Put an exhaust fan in a window to increase ventilation.

What to do with the doors?
Leave the doors hanging, unless you need to remove them to take up the old flooring. A closed door will help protect other areas of the house from dust. You can trim doors just before installing the tile or after you have laid it.

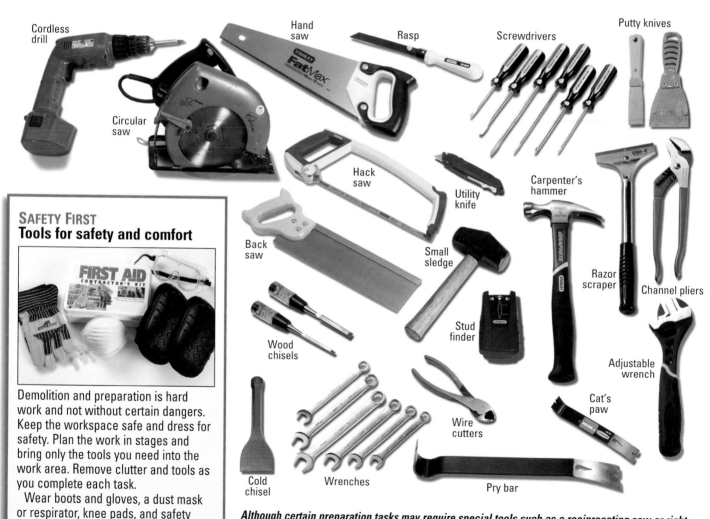

SAFETY FIRST
Tools for safety and comfort

Demolition and preparation is hard work and not without certain dangers. Keep the workspace safe and dress for safety. Plan the work in stages and bring only the tools you need into the work area. Remove clutter and tools as you complete each task.

Wear boots and gloves, a dust mask or respirator, knee pads, and safety glasses. Keep a well-stocked first-aid kit handy in case of mishaps.

Although certain preparation tasks may require special tools such as a reciprocating saw or right angled grinder, these tools will accomplish most of the work. Rent special tools at a local rental supply store and plan the work so you can return them in a day.

Tool labels: Cordless drill · Circular saw · Hand saw · Rasp · Screwdrivers · Putty knives · Hack saw · Utility knife · Carpenter's hammer · Back saw · Small sledge · Razor scraper · Channel pliers · Wood chisels · Stud finder · Adjustable wrench · Cold chisel · Wrenches · Wire cutters · Cat's paw · Pry bar

PREPARATION STEPS FOR EXISTING SURFACES

Existing surface types	Demolition	Preparation	Type of setting bed
FLOORS			
Hardwood strip or planks			
Strips/planks on wood frame	Remove if in poor repair, install new subfloor	If in good repair, stabilize and repair surface	Thinset
Strips/planks on slab	Remove flooring	Repair and roughen surface	Thinset
Carpet			
Padded carpet on slab	Remove carpet, pad, tack strip	Scrape off pad and glue; slip sheet cracks	Thinset
Glued-down carpet on slab	Remove carpet	Scrape off adhesive; slip sheet cracks	Thinset
Padded carpet on wood	Remove carpet, pad, tack strip	Glue and screw backerboard	Thinset
Resilient materials			
Vinyl on slab	Remove vinyl	Scrape off adhesives; slip sheet cracks	Thinset
Vinyl on wood	Remove vinyl that comes off easily	Glue and screw backerboard	Thinset
Ceramic tile			
Ceramic tile on slab	If loose or damaged, chip out tile	Scrape off all old setting materials; slip sheet all cracks	Thinset
Ceramic tile, mortar bed	If solid and resulting floor will not be too high, leave in	Remove loose tile and fill voids; clean and etch tile	Thinset
Ceramic tile on wood	Remove tile	Glue and screw down backerboard	Thinset
WALLS			
Drywall/plaster			
Painted	None	Degloss high sheen; scrape loose paint	Mastic/thinset
Wallpapered	Remove paper	Scrape off adhesive; clean surface	Mastic/thinset
Ceramic tile	Chip off tile	Scrape off adhesives; repair	Mastic/thinset
Ceramic tile (shower area)	Remove tile and drywall to studs	Install backerboard	Thinset
Cultured marble	Remove marble and drywall	Install backerboard	Thinset
Paneling			
Hardwood wainscoting	Remove hardwood	Repair surface	Mastic/thinset
Plywood/hardboard paneling	Remove paneling	Repair surface	Mastic/thinset

COUNTERTOPS

Removal of existing material and rebuilding new countertop base is generally preferred to installing tile over existing surface.

Removing Molding and Baseboards

In rooms without appliances, preparation of a floor for tiling begins by removing moldings and baseboards. (In kitchens and any room with appliances, remove the appliances first—see *page 42).*

Most rooms with wooden baseboards will also have a shoe molding (often called quarterround) covering the gap at the floor. Shoe moldings come off first, then the baseboards—but take the baseboard off only if you plan to finish your room with a vinyl or ceramic tile base. A reinstalled or new wood baseboard will show voids under it where it meets the tile. Those gaps are unsightly and difficult to clean, especially in kitchens and baths. So leave the baseboard in place if it is in good repair or if you're not adding a new one. When you lay the new tile, install it up to the baseboard.

If you plan to reuse the shoe molding, number the pieces as you remove them and mark the corner where you started. Shoe molding sections must go back in their original order.

Prestart Checklist

☐ **Time**
About 10 minutes total per lineal foot to remove shoe molding and wood baseboard, slightly more for cove-molding and tile removal. Nail removal and adhesive cleanup can be time-consuming and varies with the length of nails and type of adhesive used

☐ **Tools**
Utility knife, wide putty knife, pry bar, hammer, scrap wood (optional), nippers or side cutters, handsaw or back saw—tools vary with type of molding removed

☐ **Skills**
Cutting precisely with utility knife, using a hammer and pry bar; threshold removal requires using a handsaw

Removing wood shoe molding and baseboards

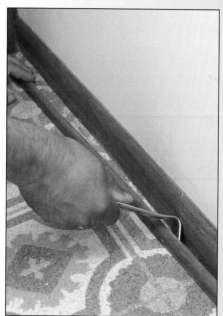

1 Starting at a corner, slide a small pry bar behind the shoe. Loosen the shoe until you can insert the pry bar next to a nail. Pry the nail out a little at a time. To avoid splits, loosen at least two nails before pulling the molding completely off the wall.

2 Begin at a corner or at a mitered joint, working a wide putty knife behind the baseboard. Loosen each nail with a pry bar. Keep the putty knife behind the bar or use a thin piece of scrap as a shim to avoid marring the surface of the wall. Loosen all nails before removing a baseboard section.

STANLEY Pro Tip: **Score the paint line**

Paint that has adhered to the wall and a wood baseboard, vinyl cove molding, or ceramic tile base may pull off the wall when you remove the molding, leaving unsightly chips that will require repainting. Repainting is time consuming, and new paint often may not match the old.

To avoid pulling the paint off the wall when removing a base molding, score the paint line with a sharp utility knife.

Insert the knife in the joint between the wall and the molding and draw the knife toward you at an angle that will follow the joint. Use enough pressure to cut through the paint. Paint can be stubborn—use two hands if necessary to cut through several coats. Make several repeated passes; the job will actually go faster and you'll avoid broken blades and skinned knuckles.

Removing vinyl cove molding

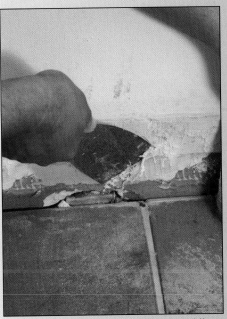

3 If you plan to reuse the shoe molding or baseboard, pull out the nails from the back. Nippers will make the job easier. Grab the nail at its base and lever it partly out. Repeat the process until the nail pops loose.

1 Insert a wide-blade putty knife at the top corner of a joint in the molding. Push down on the knife and lift the molding off the surface of the wall. Slide the full width of the blade under the molding and strip it off, keeping the knife handle parallel to the floor as much as possible.

2 When you have removed all the molding strips, use your putty knife to scrape off the remaining adhesive. Keep the knife at an angle that will remove the adhesive without gouging the wall surface. Light pressure and repeated passes work better than trying to remove the adhesive all at once.

Removing ceramic tile

Tap the pry bar into the joint. Pop each tile loose. If necessary, protect the wall with scrap behind the bar. Scrape off adhesive.

Removing thresholds

1 Use a handsaw or back saw to cut the threshold in half all the way to the surface of the floor. Cut carefully to avoid damaging other sufaces.

2 Pry each piece up with a pry bar and remove it. If the threshold is screwed down, remove the screws and slide it out from under the door trim.

REMOVING APPLIANCES

Tile must extend under appliances, such as dishwashers, compactors, and stoves, so cleaning liquids or spills and leaks won't drain over the tile edge and damage the floor below.

Remove appliances early in the preparation stage of your project so they won't be in the way when you perform the rest of the demolition, preparation, and repairs.

The space under appliances provides an excellent opportunity to use large pieces of cut tile, tiles cut inaccurately, or tiles whose glaze is flawed or whose color doesn't match the dye lot of the rest.

Before moving appliances, check to see if they will fit their enclosures after you've laid the new tile. Remember, new tile may increase the height of the floor, so measure each appliance and add the thickness of the tile and adhesive. Compare this measurement with the height of the enclosures. To make room, you may have to cut the cabinet frame above a refrigerator or raise a countertop with shims to accommodate a dishwasher *(page 69)*.

PRESTART CHECKLIST

☐ **TIME**
About 15 minutes to remove a refrigerator, 15 to 20 minutes for gas appliances and plug-in electric units, more for direct-wired appliances

☐ **TOOLS**
Channel-joint pliers, adjustable wrench, straight and phillips screwdrivers, cordless drill and bits, appliance dolly

☐ **SKILLS**
Removing screws with screwdrivers or cordless drill, removing nuts with wrenches, moving large appliances

☐ **PREP**
Shut off water-supply valves

☐ **MATERIALS**
Duct tape and wire nuts

Removing a dishwasher

Dishwasher plug

1 Unplug the dishwasher cord from the receptacle under the sink. If you don't see a power plug on the cord, the dishwasher is wired directly into the circuit and the wiring itself must be disconnected. In such installations, **shut off the power before proceeding.**

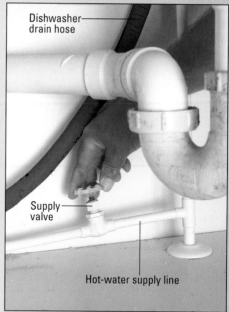

Dishwasher drain hose

Supply valve

Hot-water supply line

2 Turn off the supply valve. Disconnect the supply line and drain hose with a wrench. Some installations require removal of these lines in the dishwasher. Remove the bottom dishwasher panel for access, tug on the lines to locate their connections, and disconnect them.

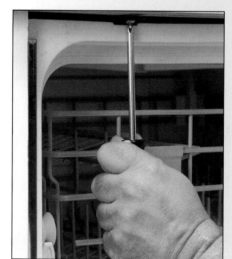

3 The dishwasher is held in the cabinet with screws fastened in the side (and on some models the top and bottom) flanges. Open the dishwasher door for access to the screws and remove them with the appropriate screwdriver or cordless drill.

4 Close the door of the dishwasher and lock it. Grasp the dishwasher by the sides of the door and/or the door handle and slide it forward. Lift up slightly and rock the unit from side to side if it sticks. If necessary, have a helper thread supply and drain lines back through the cabinet holes as you pull.

Removing a countertop range

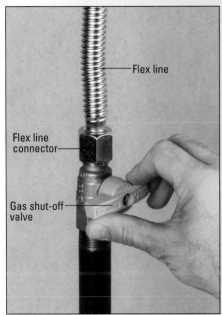

Flex line

Flex line connector

Gas shut-off valve

1 For a gas unit, **shut off the gas** by turning the handle on the shutoff valve. Using channel-joint pliers, loosen the flex-line connector and disconnect the line from the valve. For an electric range, **unplug the 220-volt power plug** under the cabinet.

2 Your range may be anchored by clips or retainers similar to those used to anchor a countertop sink *(page 67)*. Remove any clips or retainers, push up on the unit from below with one hand to create a space for lifting, then lift the unit up and out. Do not kink the flex line; kinking may put holes in it.

WHAT IF...
An electric appliance is wired directly to the circuit?

Circuit breaker

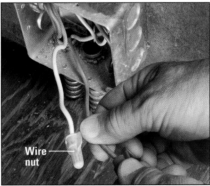

Wire nut

If you don't see a plug on the power cord of an appliance, the unit is wired directly to a circuit. **Turn off the circuit breaker** and tape a note to it so someone doesn't turn it on accidentally. Find the junction box to which the appliance is connected; remove the cover plate. **Use a voltage tester to check the**

wires for power. If they are dead, disconnect the wires, noting how they are attached. Loosen the cord clamp on the side of the box and pull out the appliance cord. Screw wire nuts tightly onto the circuit wires and tuck them into the box. Attach the cover plate. **If in doubt, call a professional electrician.**

Removing a stove

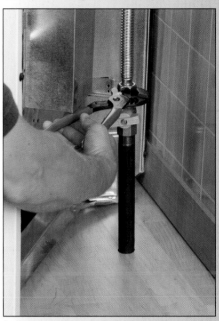

Pull the stove away from the wall enough to reach the power plug or gas valve. **Unplug the power cord or turn off the gas valve.** Using channel-joint pliers, loosen the flex-line connector. Bend the flex line gently and tape it out of the way. Dolly the stove to a different room.

SAFETY FIRST
Use an appliance dolly

An appliance dolly moves heavy items safely. Slide the dolly plate under the unit, tighten the strap, tip the unit back slightly, and roll it away. Enlist a helper to move large appliances.

REMOVING FIXTURES

Although you can leave toilets and sinks in place and tile around them, removing them makes the job easier. With the fixtures out of the way, you'll have more working room, substantially fewer cut tiles to install, and fewer exposed joints to maintain. You'll spend less time removing fixtures than cutting tiles, and the result will be much more attractive and professional looking.

For tub and shower fixtures, removal is not an option. These fixtures must come off before you tile the wall around them.

Over time, fixture anchor bolts can rust, bend, and otherwise undergo alterations that can make their removal a stubborn chore. A few special techniques (*page 45*) will quickly solve these problems.

PRESTART CHECKLIST

☐ **TIME**
About 30 to 45 minutes each for toilet, wall-mounted sink, and pedestal sink (more if anchor bolts prove stubborn); about 15 minutes for tub and shower fixture set

☐ **TOOLS**
Plumber's plunger, channel-joint pliers, locking pliers (optional), adjustable wrench, straight and phillips screwdrivers, allen wrenches, narrow putty knife, carpenter's hammer (optional), hacksaw, mini-hacksaw (optional), pipe wrench, tape measure

☐ **PREP**
Turn off water supply valve(s) for each fixture removed

☐ **SKILLS**
Removing screws with screwdrivers, removing fasteners with wrenches

☐ **MATERIALS**
Bleach, rags, plastic bag, penetrating oil, several wood shims, repair ring, new closet flange and bolts, duct tape, pipe nipples and caps

Removing a toilet

Water supply line
Supply-line nut
Shutoff valve

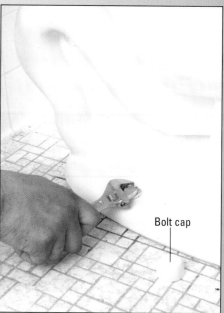

Bolt cap

1 Pour a quart of bleach into the tank, flush, and let it refill. Close the supply valve and reflush, holding the handle down until the tank empties. Push the water out of the trap with a plunger and stuff the bowl with rags. Disconnect the supply line with a wrench or channel-joint pliers.

2 Pry off the anchor bolt caps. Remove the anchor bolts with an adjustable wrench or channel-joint pliers. If the bolts spin, snap, or won't come off, try one of the solutions below. Even if you have to cut the bolts, you can still remove the toilet and replace the bolts when you reinstall it.

TYPICAL TOILET INSTALLATION

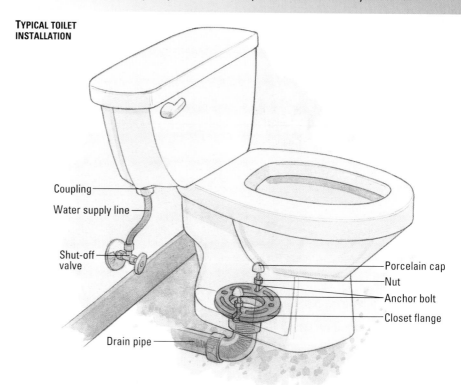

Coupling
Water supply line
Shut-off valve
Drain pipe

Porcelain cap
Nut
Anchor bolt
Closet flange

3 The bottom of the toilet trap fits snugly over a wax ring that seals it against the closet flange in the floor (see illustration below). To break the seal of the wax ring, rock the toilet gently back and forth as you lift it off the floor. Newer, low-capacity toilets may be light enough for you to lift by yourself, but older toilets can weigh up to 60 pounds. Get help to avoid risk of injury. Lift the toilet off the floor and carry it to another room.

4 With one hand in a plastic bag, grab the inside bottom edge of the ring. Pull it out, pulling the bag over the ring with your other hand. Dispose of the ring. With a putty knife scrape residue from the flange. Stuff a large rag into the drain to keep out debris. Measure from the flange to the height of the new tile (the combined thickness of new tile and backerboard). Purchase a flange extender, if necessary, to bring the flange about ¼ inch above the new floor.

WHAT IF ...
Toilet bolts spin, snap, or won't come off?

If the bolts snap when you try to remove the nut, pull out the broken piece, remove the toilet, and see if the pieces remaining in the flange will come loose with locking pliers. If they won't, you can install a repair flange before you begin tiling the floor.

If a bolt spins, drive a wood shim under the toilet on both sides of the bolt. The resulting upward pressure may keep it from spinning so you can unscrew the nut.

Stubborn nuts may loosen with a squirt of penetrating oil. Let the oil set for about 10 minutes before again trying to loosen the nuts.

If a nut still won't budge or if the wood shims didn't stop the bolt from spinning, saw the bolt with a hacksaw. Insert the hacksaw blade under the nut and cut through the bolt. If there isn't enough working room for a full-sized saw, use a minihacksaw (as shown).

Install a flange extension

The combined thickness of new flooring materials—cement board, thinset, and tile—may raise the floor by as much as 1 inch. Raise the height of the flange with an extender.

Available at most hardware stores, an extender consists of rings that are stacked over the floor flange and sealed with silicone caulk. Add enough rings to bring the flange at least flush with and preferably about ¼ inch higher than the new floor.

Removing a showerhead

1 If you are replacing the plumbing or valves to a shower, you must first turn off the water supply. Remove the showerhead with an adjustable or open-end wrench. If the showerhead is not machined for a wrench, use channel-joint pliers, protecting the collar with duct tape or rags.

2 Wrap the gooseneck with several layers of duct tape about 1 inch from the wall to protect it. Adjust a pipe wrench so it just fits over the gooseneck and position the jaws so the wrench will pull counter-clockwise. Pull the wrench firmly, keeping it perpendicular to the pipe.

TYPICAL SHOWER INSTALLATION

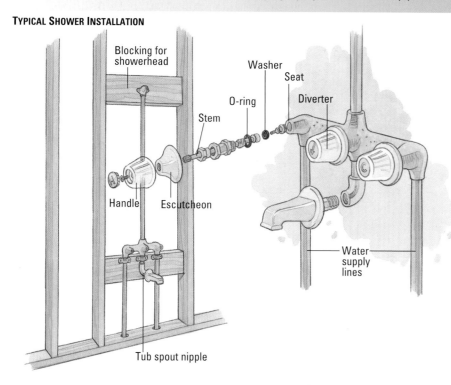

Blocking for showerhead

Washer

Seat

O-ring

Diverter

Stem

Handle

Escutcheon

Water supply lines

Tub spout nipple

Removing a tub spout

Grasp the spout firmly with both hands and unscrew it from the fitting. If the spout is fastened to the pipe with a clamp, loosen the clamp screw—usually accessible from the plumbing access door on the other side of the wall behind the shower. Pull off the spout.

SHOWER AND TUB FITTINGS
Cap the pipe

Once you have removed a shower gooseneck or tub spout, screw a pipe nipple into the fitting. A nipple is a 5- to 6-inch length of water pipe threaded on one end and capped on the other. It temporarily replaces the fixture and allows you to cut the backerboard in the exact location for the pipe. It also protects the fitting threads from becoming clogged with adhesive. Take the gooseneck or tub spout to the hardware store so you find the right nipple size.

Removing shower faucet handles

1 Most faucets fit on a valve stem and are held in place with set screws. If the screw is not visible, you'll find it under a cover plate. Insert a thin screwdriver blade under the edge of the cover plate and use slight pressure to pop it off. Cover the drain to make sure you don't lose the screw.

2 Select the proper size screwdriver (usually a phillips head) and remove the screws from each faucet.

3 Grasp the handle from the back—with both hands if necessary—and pull it toward you. Wiggling the handle sometimes helps. Penetrating oil also helps. If the handle is especially stubborn, rent a special tool called a handle puller. Tape all the parts together and store them out of the way.

STANLEY PRO TIP

Measure the thread length

If you are tiling over existing wall tile or installing new tile with backerboard, the combined thickness of the new materials may exceed the length of the threads on your faucet valves. The threads of the valves need to extend beyond the new wall.

Measure the depth of the threads. If they are less than the thickness of the new materials, you'll have to install new faucets—a job best left to a plumber.

WHAT IF …
A faucet has only one handle?

Plastic screw cap

Escutcheon plate

1 Remove the set screw (on the underside of the handle or under a plastic cap) with a screwdrive or allen wrench. If you can't find a set screw, try unscrewing the handle itself.

2 Pull the handle off the stem and remove the escutcheon-plate screws. Pull off the escutcheon plate and any other plates under it, tape the parts together, and store them.

Removing a pedestal sink

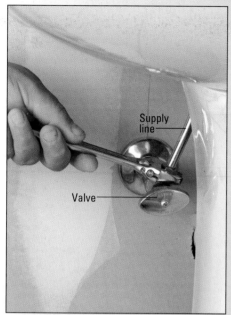

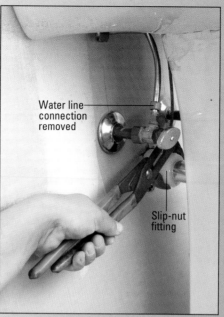

1 Shut off both the hot and cold water valves and loosen the compression nuts on both supply lines with a wrench or channel-joint pliers. Pull the supply line out of the valve. If the sink has fixed-length supply lines, remove the nut and push the lines gently out of the way.

2 Place a pile of rags under the trap to catch any water released as you remove the pipe. Loosen the slip-nut fitting (on both ends of the trap, if possible) with channel-joint pliers or a pipe wrench and pull the trap off. Pour the trap water in a bucket.

3 Remove any bolts attaching the top to the pedestal. Lift the top off. If the sink is hung on wall brackets, grasp it near the wall and pull up. Unbolt the pedestal from the floor and lift it off. If the pedestal is a one-piece unit, unbolt it from the wall and floor. Remove the wall brackets if tiling the wall.

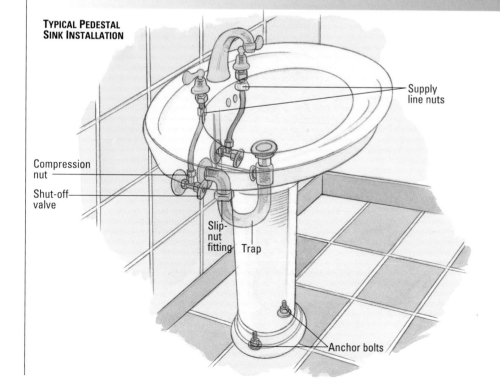

TYPICAL PEDESTAL SINK INSTALLATION

Supply line nuts

Compression nut

Shut-off valve

Slip-nut fitting Trap

Anchor bolts

Tiling around floor pipes

Many steam and hot-water heating systems that use baseboard elements and floor-standing radiators have delivery pipes that come up through the floor. When you lay your floor tile around these pipes, tile to within ¼ inch of them and fill the gap with silicone caulk instead of grout. The caulk will let the pipes move in the hole without making noise.

Remove floor radiators for floor-tile installations and when tiling a wall behind them. Wall-mounted heating elements can be left in place when tiling a wall, but the job will look neater if you remove them.

In either case, shut off the heat supply and disconnect the unit at the outflow side of the valve. Steam and hot-water system fittings can be stubborn. Use a pipe wrench or enlist the services of a professional.

Removing a wall-mounted sink

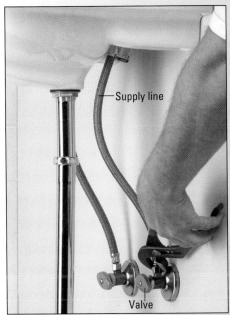

Supply line

Valve

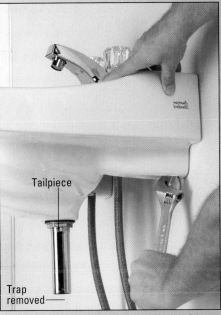

Tailpiece

Trap removed

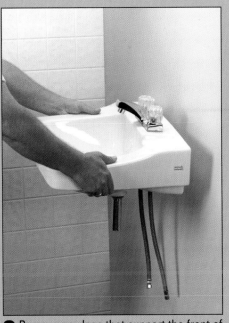

1 Shut off both the hot and cold water valves and loosen the compression nuts on both supply lines with channel-joint pliers or a wrench. Pull the supply line out of the valve. If you have fixed-length supply lines, remove the compression nut and move the lines out of the way.

2 Set a bucket under the trap to catch any water released as you remove the pipe. Loosen the slip-nut fittings on both ends of the trap with channel-joint pliers or a pipe wrench and pull the trap off the tailpiece. Dump the trap water in the bucket and remove the sink mounting bolts.

3 Remove any legs that support the front of the sink. Grasp the sink with both hands near the wall and pull it up and off the brackets. If the sink won't come loose, try loosening the wall-bracket bolts a couple of turns and then pull the sink off the brackets. Remove the brackets if tiling the wall.

Tiling around electrical boxes

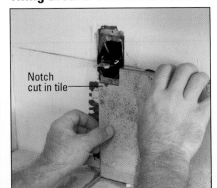

Notch cut in tile

Turn off the power to the box, remove its cover plate, and push the receptacle or switch into the box. When you tile the wall, notch the tiles around the box and use longer screws to reattach the receptacle or switch. Reattach the cover plate. Turn on the power when the job is done.

TYPICAL WALL-MOUNTED SINK INSTALLATION

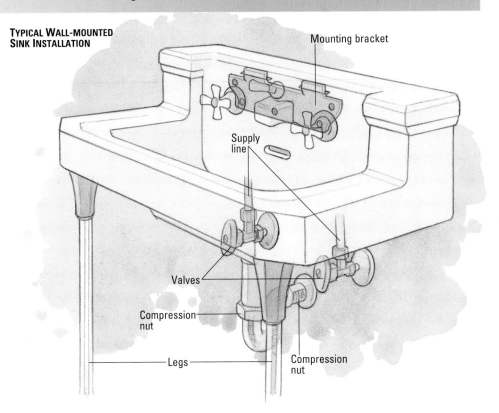

Mounting bracket

Supply line

Valves

Compression nut

Legs

Compression nut

REPAIRING OR REMOVING THE EXISTING FLOOR

When preparing your floor for tile, first decide whether to remove the existing flooring or repair it and tile over it.

Carpet, of course, must be removed, but you can lay tile over hardwood flooring and ceramic tile—if the surface and subfloor are stable and in good condition, and if the new tile and materials won't raise the floor by more than ¾ inch. The same is true for uncushioned resilient tile or sheet materials on a wood frame floor. Remove cushioned resilients; the tile weight can compress them and cause cracks. Don't lay tile directly on resilients. Lay backerboard first (page 72). Always remove resilients from a concrete slab before installing tile.

Removing the existing floor will minimize any change in floor levels and will reveal any hidden faults that need repair.

PRESTART CHECKLIST

☐ **TIME**
From 30 to 45 minutes per square yard to repair or remove flooring; total time will vary with size of project

☐ **TOOLS**
Wood floors—framing square, circular saw, chisels, pry bar, hammer, cordless drill, plug cutter (optional)
Resilient floors—heat gun, wide putty knife, floor scraper, utility knife
Carpet—utility knife, pry bar, hammer, screwdriver, floor scraper
Ceramic tile—cold chisels, hammer, margin trowel, sanding block

☐ **SKILLS**
Prying with pry bar, removing and driving fasteners with screwdrivers and cordless drill, cutting with circular saw

☐ **MATERIALS**
Wood flooring: ¾-inch exterior plywood
Resilient flooring: adhesive remover, thinset mortar
Ceramic tile: thinset mortar, extra tile

Repairing damaged hardwood flooring

1 Use a framing square and carpenter's pencil to outline the edge of the damaged area. Set a circular saw to the depth of the hardwood flooring, start the saw with only the front edge of the saw plate resting on the floor, and lower the blade into the cut. Repeat along each line.

2 Chisel out enough flooring to let you insert a prybar under the flooring. Tap the pry bar under the strips or planks at a nail and pry it up. Repeat the process at each nail location within the damaged area. Dispose of the flooring you have removed.

Removing a hardwood floor

1 Using the techniques shown above for repairing damaged flooring, make several plunge cuts in one or two strips or planks. Chisel out the cut area.

2 Tap a pry bar under the flooring at each nail and pry the material up, working along the length of each board. Insert the bar fully under the strip or plank, not the tongue. Otherwise, you will split the tongue off the flooring and not remove the strip.

Secure loose planks or strips

3 Measure the area you have removed and cut a piece of ¾-inch exterior-grade plywood to the same dimensions. Fit the plywood into the recess, and using a cordless drill, drive 1⅜-inch coated screws at 3- to 4-inch intervals through the plywood and into the subfloor. Countersink the screws slightly. If your hardwood floor has been refinished, the patch might be thicker than the floor. Use a belt sander to sand the patch till it's level with the flooring.

Floor tile requires a level, firm surface. Anchor any loose hardwood flooring securely. Walk the floor and mark areas that feel spongy or loose. Fasten loose boards at their edges with ringshank or spiral shank nails, or use a cordless drill and drive 1⅜-inch coated screws through the hardwood and into the subfloor. Predrill the holes to avoid splitting the material.

WHAT IF ...
Flooring is plugged plank or parquet?

Use an oversize plug cutter bit in a drill to remove one plug. If no screw is present, the plugs are decorative and don't need removal. Take up the flooring as shown on *page 50*.

If you find screws under the plug, cut out all plugs and remove the screws using a cordless drill. Then take up the flooring using the techniques shown.

Tap the blade of a wide chisel under the edge of one parquet tile and pry the tile loose. Repeat for each tile and scrape up the adhesive with a wide putty knife.

STANLEY PRO TIP

Reduce the elevation

The combined thickness of new tile and adhesive installed on an existing hardwood floor can raise the height of the floor by more than ¾ inch. Such an elevation can cause awkward or unsafe transitions between the new floor and the adjoining surface.

When laying tile over hardwood flooring, you can ease such abrupt transitions by using ¼-inch cement backerboard instead of the usual ½-inch thickness. The stability of the hardwood when properly prepared and the subfloor underneath will provide sufficient strength for any floor tile or stone.

Removing resilient tile

Warm the adhesive with a heat gun. If you don't have a heat gun, use a hair dryer set on high heat. Warm a corner first, insert a floor scraper or wide putty knife, and with the heat on, lift up the tile. Scrape the adhesive from the floor with a floor scraper.

Removing resilient sheet flooring

1 Start at a corner or at a bubbled seam. Insert a floor scraper or wide putty knife under the sheet flooring and pry it up. Work down each strip of the material, rolling the strip as you go. If the material is unbacked, use a hair dryer or heat gun to soften the adhesive as you go.

2 Once you have removed the sheet flooring, spray the surface in sections with adhesive remover. Let the remover work according to the manufacturer's instructions, then use a wide scraper or putty knife to peel the residue from the floor.

Repairing resilient surfaces

If you are tiling over a resilient surface on a wood subfloor, and the resilient material is damaged in only a few sections, you can repair it rather than remove it completely.

Using a utility knife, cut through the damaged area to the subfloor. Remove the damaged tile(s) or section(s) of sheet material with a wide putty knife or scraper. Scrape the remaining adhesive from the floor within the area.

Using a mason's trowel or a margin trowel, smear the recess with thinset mortar and level it. Let this thinset dry before applying backerboard.

Use this patching method only on resilient material over a wood frame floor. Always remove resilients from slab before tiling.

STANLEY PRO TIP

Strips make it easier

Stripping and removing room-sized sections of resilient sheet flooring or carpet is time-consuming and heavy work. To make the job easier, cut resilient sheet flooring or carpet into 12-inch strips before you pull or scrape it up.

SAFETY FIRST
Asbestos warning

Before you remove any resilient material, check with a professional to determine if it contains asbestos.

Asbestos was used as a binder in most resilient flooring materials prior to 1985 and its fibers have since been found to be a carcinogen, especially dangerous when inhaled. Virtually no material installed prior to 1985 can be assured to be asbestos-free. It was used in asphalt tile, linoleum, vinyl-asbestos tile and sheet flooring, and asphalt "cutback" adhesives.

If possible, leave asbestos flooring in place and install underlayment or backerboard over it. Never sand, dry-scrape, or dry-sweep any materials with asbestos content. Contract with a professional for removal of asbestos flooring. Look in the phone directory under "Asbestos Removal."

Removing conventional carpet

1 Pry up all metal edgings at doorways. If the carpet is not tacked or glued to the floor, work a straight screwdriver under a corner or grab the corner with channel-joint pliers and pull each strip of carpet off the tackless strip. Once you get started, the carpet should tear up easily.

2 If the pad didn't get cut through when you cut the carpet in strips, recut the pad with a utility knife. Then grab each section of pad with both hands and pull it from the floor. Roll the pad as you go and dispose of the rolls. Remove pad tacks or staples.

3 Starting at a joint in the tackless strip, work the end of a pry bar under the strip at a nail and pry the nail loose. Use care and wear gloves when carrying the strips to a refuse pile or garbage bin—the points of the tacks are sharp.

WHAT IF ...
The carpet or pad is tacked or stapled?

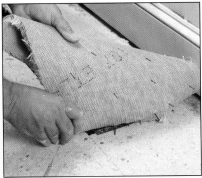

To remove tacked carpet, pry up a few tacks with a screwdriver or cat's paw and try to pull the carpet up. If that doesn't work, pull up each tack or staple separately.
   Remove pad staples and any remaining tufts of pad with a screwdriver or cat's paw.

WHAT IF ...
Carpet is glued down?

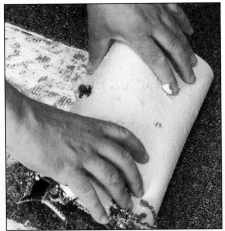

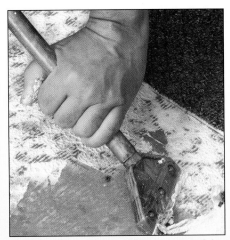

1 Starting at a corner or along one edge of a cut strip, drive a wide putty knife or scraper between the backing and the floor to break the adhesive bond. Roll up the carpet as you go.

2 Once you have removed and disposed of the carpet, go back and scrape up the remaining tufts of pad and adhesive residue with a floor scraper.

Using existing floor tile as substrate

1 Existing tile can be used as a substrate. Start by repairing any damaged sections. Remove the grout from the damaged tile with a grout knife. With a high-quality hammer or small sledge and cold chisel, break the tile, working from the center to the edges. **Wear eye protection.**

2 Pull out the chips of broken tile. Scrape up the fine pieces with a margin trowel or putty knife. Using the same tool, scrape off any adhesive remaining in the recess. Dust out or vacuum the area so the thinset can bond securely with the floor.

3 Using a margin trowel or wide putty knife, apply adhesive in the recess. If possible, use the same general type of adhesive as the original mastic or thinset.

Removing floor tile set in thinset

1 Create a starting point in a central area of the floor by cracking one tile with a small sledge and cold chisel. Grip the chisel firmly and strike it with a sharp blow of the hammer. **Be sure to wear eye protection.**

2 Break out the remaining area of the tile with the sledge and brush the loose pieces out of the recess. Chip out the grout along the edge of an adjacent tile.

3 Tap a wide chisel at an angle under the edge of the adjoining tile and pop off the tile. Repeat the process for each tile until you have removed the entire floor. Dispose of the tile and scrape off any remaining adhesive.

4 Back-butter a replacement tile using a margin trowel or putty knife and push the tile into the recess until the adhesive oozes up from the grout joints. Make sure the tile is level with the rest of the floor, wipe off the excess thinset, and let it cure.

5 Use a sanding block and a coarse grit of abrasive paper to roughen the entire surface of the tile. This will give the tile a "tooth" for the adhesive and strengthen its bond with the floor.

6 With a margin trowel or mason's trowel spread a thin layer of thinset across the entire surface of the floor. Make sure that the grout joints are level with the surface of the tile.

WHAT IF ...
Tile is set in a mortar bed?

For centuries, craftspeople set tile in a bed of mortar, which resulted in an extremely durable installation. Mortar-bed tile will consequently prove more difficult to remove than tile set in thinset adhesive. If your mortar-bed floor is essentially stable and sound with all or most of the tiles securely adhered—and if the new tile surface won't extend above the adjacent floors to an unsafe height—you can install new tile over the old.

If the existing surface is cracked or in disrepair, or if the resulting floor will be too high, chip off the tile using the techniques shown for a thinset installation. You can also break the bed with a sledge hammer or saw it into sections with a diamond masonry saw and pry the sections out with a crowbar.

In either case, you will have to remove the mortar bed and prepare the floor for thinset.

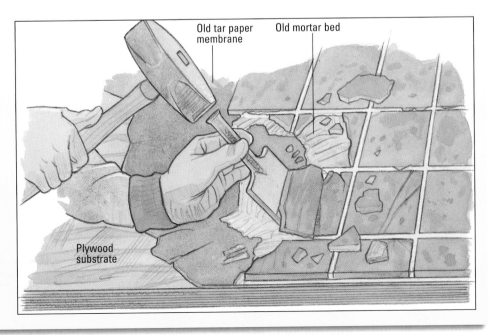

Old tar paper membrane

Old mortar bed

Plywood substrate

PREPARING A WOOD SUBFLOOR

After you have removed or repaired the existing surface of the floor, turn your attention to the subfloor. To keep the tile from cracking, subfloors must be free of squeaks, sags, and other imperfections. Inspect the subfloor and make repairs that will assure it provides a solid, stable bed.

Dimensional lumber, such as 1×4 or 2×6 planking, is not suitable as a tile setting bed. Plank flooring expands and contracts rapidly with changes in temperature and humidity. Tile does not. The result can be cracked tile and broken grout joints. Install backerboard on plank *(page 74)*. If the resulting floor will be too high for smooth transitions to adjacent floors, tear up the planking and install ¾-inch exterior plywood, followed by backerboard.

Vacuum and damp-mop the surface.

PRESTART CHECKLIST

☐ **TIME**
About 30 minutes to check defects in an average size room. Repair time will vary with size and condition of floor, could average 45 minutes per square yard.

☐ **TOOLS**
Repair subfloor: 4-foot level, cordless drill/bits, hammer, circular saw
Repairing surface: mason's trowel, belt sander
Installing membrane: roller, mason's trowel

☐ **SKILLS**
Driving nails with hammer, removing fasteners with cordless drill, sawing with circular saw

☐ **PREP**
Remove or repair finished flooring

☐ **MATERIALS**
Subfloor: 2×4 lumber, 2½-inch coated screws, 8d nails, wood shims
Surface: thinset mortar
Installing membrane: membrane and adhesive

1 Divide the floor into imaginary 6-foot sections and within each section, rotate a 4-foot level. Use a carpenter's pencil or chalk marker to outline sags, low spots, high spots, and other defects. Then walk the floor to test it for squeaks and weak spots. Mark these areas.

2×4 bridging

2 If the entire subfloor is weak, cut 2×4 bridges to fit between the floor joists. Measure the joist spacing across the floor and if the dimensions are equal cut all the bridges at one time. If the spacing varies, cut the pieces to fit. Nail the bridges in place, offsetting each one by 24 inches.

WHAT IF ...
Floor has low or high spots?

Vacuum the floor thoroughly. Trowel thinset into depressions and chips with a mason's trowel or margin trowel. Feather the edges of the repair so it is level with the floor. After it dries, sand the edges of the repair if necessary.

Before you level any high spots on the floor, make sure the heads of all nails and fasteners are set below the surface. Level high spots on the floor with a belt sander. Keep the sander moving when it is in contact with the floor.

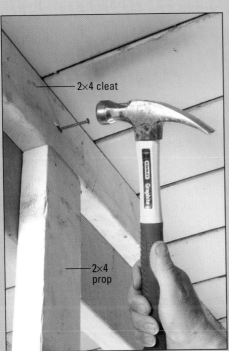

3 Shore up broken or sagging joists by nailing a 2×4 cleat up against the subfloor. Force the cleat snugly against the subfloor with a 2×4 prop, nail the cleat in place with 8d nails, and knock the prop out to remove it.

4 Fill minor sags and separations between the subfloor and joists by driving shims or shingles into the gap. Tap the shim gently until it's snug—forcing it may cause the flooring above to bow.

5 Fasten loose subflooring material securely by screwing it to the joists. Drive screws into any repairs you have made with shims. You can use ring-shank or spiral-shank nails as an alternative, setting the nailhead below the surface with a hammer and nail set.

STANLEY PRO TIP

Support the stone

Because stone tiles are more brittle than ceramic tile, they won't forgive unstable subfloors or surfaces that are not flat. Stone installations require subfloor support that is solid and free from deflection. Substrates also must be smooth and level.

When preparing a subfloor for stone tile, be thorough and precise when marking defects such as high spots or depressions. Finish the edges of thinset repairs with care and make sure you have removed all structural defects in the joists and subfloor.

Stone is substantially heavier than tile, and current flooring, especially in large rooms, may not be strong enough to support it. Check with a structural engineer if you are in doubt.

Waterproofing membrane

Although many tiles and setting materials are impervious to water, virtually no tile installation should be thought of as completely waterproof without a waterproofing membrane.

Water that penetrates grout joints or the edges of tile can weaken the adhesive, promote rot, and nourish organisms destructive to the wood subfloor.

Bathrooms, kitchens, and surfaces that require frequent cleaning are especially vulnerable.

One of the easiest membranes to apply utilizes an adhesive that spreads with a roller. To install it, start at a wall opposite a doorway and apply the adhesive in sections with a roller (top). Let the adhesive cure, spread the fiber membrane over it (middle), and retrowel the membrane into the adhesive (bottom).

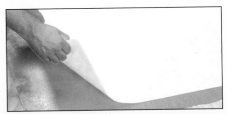

PREPARING A SLAB FLOOR

Water is the chief enemy of all building materials. Slab floors, especially those at or below grade, are especially vulnerable. Don't tile until you fix water problems.

Condensation on water pipes and walls occurs in hot weather and is not technically a water problem. Relieve condensation by increasing ventilation.

Install or fix gutters and slope soil away from the foundation so water runs away from it. If this doesn't fix the problem, consult a drainage specialist.

Cover isolated, inactive cracks with an isolation membrane "bandage." Completely cover new concrete and any floors suspected of developing cracks. Fix active cracks before tiling—don't cover them up.

PRESTART CHECKLIST

☐ **TIME**
From 30 to 45 minutes per square yard

☐ **TOOLS**
Repair or degloss surface—level, hammer, cold chisel, margin and mason's trowels, grinder, sanding block, brush
Repair structural defect—sledge, crowbar, wheelbarrow
Install membrane—roller, mason's trowel

☐ **SKILLS**
Using a level, troweling, grinding with power grinder

☐ **PREP**
Remove or repair finished flooring

☐ **MATERIALS**
Repair/degloss surface—thinset, muriatic acid, rubber gloves
Repair structural defect—gravel, reinforcing wire, epoxy bonding agent, concrete mix, 2×4 screed
Install membrane—membrane and adhesive

1 Divide the slab into imaginary 6-foot sections and check each section with a 4-foot level. Mark cracks, high spots, and other defects with a carpenter's pencil.

Cracks may be a sign of a structural defect. Some may be repairable. Others may require professional help.

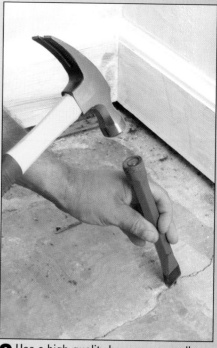

2 Use a high-quality hammer or small sledge and a cold chisel to open small cracks so you can fill them. If possible, angle the chisel into each side of the crack to create a recess wider at the bottom of the crack than on top. This will help hold the patching cement more securely.

WHAT IF …
A slab is waxed, sealed, or smooth-finished?

Thinset and other adhesives will not bind to surfaces that are waxed, sealed, painted, or finished to a gloss with a steel trowel. You can tell if your slab is waxed or sealed if spilled water beads up on it. If water soaks in and the surface is otherwise slick and smooth, it is likely to have been finished with a steel trowel.

Roughen slick or painted finishes with a sanding block or rented floor sander. Make your own sanding block by tacking a sheet of coarse abrasive on an 8-inch 2×4. Use light pressure and scuff the entire floor. Vacuum the floor when finished.

Remove wax and sealers with a solution of 4 parts water to 1 part muriatic acid. Scour the floor with the acid wash and a scrub brush. Rinse the slab with clear water and let it dry thoroughly.

Muriatic acid is highly caustic. Follow the manufacturer's directions and wear eye protection, rubber gloves, and old clothing. Ventilate the area.

3 Wash out the crack with water and fill it with quick-setting hydraulic cement or thinset. Use a margin trowel or mason's trowel and feather out the edges until the patch is level with the surrounding surface.

4 To fill depressions in the slab, pour a small amount of thinset or self-leveling compound into the depression and trowel it level. Add thinset or compound until the surface is level and feather the edges of thinset even with the floor.

5 Grind down any high spots you have marked with a grinder equipped with a masonry-grit abrasive wheel. A right-angled grinder makes this job go quickly. Hold a vacuum hose near the grinder to remove the dust as you work. Vacuum and damp-mop the surface thoroughly.

Structural defects in concrete

Large holes, cracks with uneven surfaces, and sunken areas are signs of structural defects in a slab. You must repair these defects before tiling.

For most repairs, the concrete will have to be broken into manageable pieces and removed. The remaining hole must be excavated by an additional 4 inches and filled with a 4-inch gravel layer. New concrete calls for reinforcing wire and screeding (leveling) with a long 2×4. The patch must cure for three to seven days.

Fixing structural defects in a slab is a formidable job. Consult with a specialist before tackling the job yourself. Contracting the work is often more cost-effective.

Apply an isolation membrane (slip sheet) over cracks

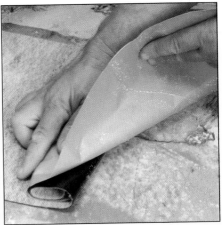

1 Apply the membrane adhesive equally on both sides of a crack or expansion joint (page 24). Use a roller to apply the adhesive and spread on a light but even coat.

2 Follow the manufacturer's instructions to apply the membrane to cured or wet adhesive. Apply the membrane over the adhesive, following the contour of the crack across the surface.

PREPARING WALLS FOR TILE

Tiled walls need to be reasonably straight, flat, and plumb before tiling. Remove any wallpaper or covering and degloss paint before you check for and repair other structural or surface defects. Do not strip paint with chemical removers. Paint stripping is unnecessary and may leave a residue that interferes with the tile adhesive.

Check the structural integrity of the wall by pushing between the studs. Drive screws into the studs to anchor soft spots where plaster or drywall has come loose.

Look for bows in the walls and crumbling surfaces. Fill in depressions, remove loose material, and repair holes. Although you can tile over a tiled wall, it is safer to remove it. Always remove tile from walls in wet locations, such as baths. Vacuum and damp sponge the surface thoroughly.

PRESTART CHECKLIST

☐ **TIME**
About 20 to 30 minutes per square yard, longer to remove wallpaper

☐ **TOOLS**
Repairing and removing drywall and plaster—level, hammer, cold chisel, framing square, margin and mason's trowels, grinder (plaster removal only)
Preparing covered walls—wide putty knife, sanding block
Removing tile—grout knife, wide cold chisel, hammer

☐ **SKILLS**
Cutting with utility knife, driving fasteners with cordless drill, troweling patching compound

☐ **MATERIALS**
Repairing/removing drywall/plaster: ¾-inch drywall, 3× lumber, 1-inch drywall screws, drywall tape, thinset, 2×4 lumber
Preparing covered walls: deglossing agent, adhesive release agent, TSP

Repairing damaged drywall

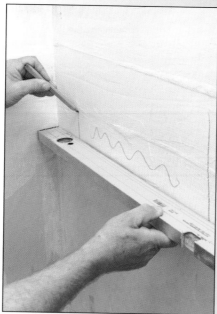

1 Push on the wall at various places to make sure it is firmly anchored to the studs. Mark places that give when you push on them. Using a 4-foot level, mark major depressions, high spots, and corners that are not plumb.

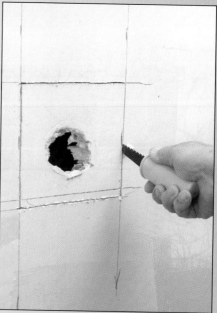

2 Use a framing square to mark a rectangular area around a hole. Score the drywall on the lines and then cut through it with a drywall saw or utility knife. Pry out the damaged area or knock it into the wall recess.

WHAT IF . . .
Walls are painted, papered, or tiled?

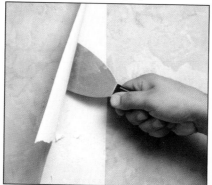

Scrape loose paint and roughen with #80 sandpaper. You can also degloss paint with a deglossing agent compatible with thinset.

To remove wallpaper, spray on a release agent. Scrape the wall with a wide putty knife. Wash the surface with a solution of trisodium-phosphate (TSP) and water.

To remove wall tiles, start at the top and remove the grout around one tile with a grout knife or saw. Tap a chisel under the tile and pop it off. Repeat for the remaining tiles, working down the wall. In wet areas, remove drywall or damaged greenboard to the studs. In dry areas, repair the wall surface.

3 Cut 1×3 boards about 6 inches longer than the area to be patched. Insert the boards into the recess on one side of the patch area and cinch them to the rear of the drywall with 1-inch screws. Repeat for the other side. These cleats will keep the drywall patch from falling into the wall.

4 Cut a drywall patch of the same thickness as the rest of the wall and to the dimensions of the repair area. Place it in the recess against the cleats. Use 1-inch screws to fasten the patch to the cleats. Tape the joint around the patch with fiberglass-mesh drywall tape.

5 Finish the joints by applying a thin coat of drywall compound or thinset. Although the edges do not have to be perfectly smooth because you will be covering them with tile adhesive, do not leave any prominent high spots of drywall compound or thinset. Sand smooth if necessary.

STANLEY PRO TIP

How to find studs in wall

Certain repairs or installations require finding studs behind a finished wall. Electronic stud finders make the job easy. Be sure to mark both edges of each stud.

If you don't have a stud finder, probe the wall by tapping a long finishing nail through the wallboard until you find both edges of one stud. Mark its center. The remaining studs should be installed at 16- or 24-inch intervals.

DRYWALL PATCH
Cutting drywall

1 Mark a line at the length or width of the cut. Using a utility knife and a straight edge on long cuts, score one side of the drywall through the paper surface and slightly into the gypsum core. You do not need to cut all the way through or even deeply into the core.

2 Turn the drywall piece over and support it, if necessary, either on the floor or on a flat surface. Break the piece along the scored line with a sharp blow of your palm. This will leave the paper backing intact on one side. Working from the unscored side, insert a utility knife through the paper backing and cut the two pieces free.

Repairing holes in plaster

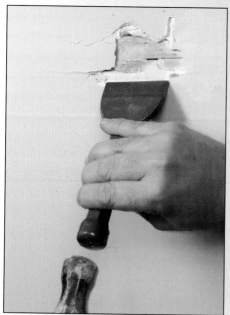

1 Cut damaged pieces from the hole with a wide cold chisel. Plaster is held together with a fibrous binder, so there may be small pieces clinging to the edge of the hole. Remove them and, if possible, angle the edges of the hole so they are wider next to the lath than at the surface.

2 Brush out the area or vacuum it. Using a spray bottle, moisten the edges of the hole and the lath with water. Don't soak the area; a moderate misting is sufficient.

3 Apply patching plaster or thinset to the damaged area with a wide putty knife, forcing the material slightly into the lath. If the thickness of the plaster is more than ½ inch, apply a thin coat first, let it dry, and apply another coat. Thick patches tend to dry with cracks if applied all at once.

Repairing an outside corner

Using a wide cold chisel, pry out the loose plaster. Clean the edges thoroughly, making sure to remove small pieces still attached with the binding material. Tack a 2×4 batten on one wall flush with the corner. Moisten the damaged area with water, and apply patching plaster or thinset in two applications, allowing one coat to dry before applying the other. Let the compound dry, move the batten to the other wall, and repeat the process. Sand smooth when dry.

Repairing cracked plaster

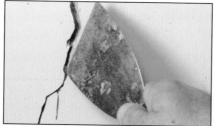

1 If the crack is a hairline crack, clean it out with the edge of a putty knife or can opener and dust out the crack with an old paint brush. Moisten the crack and apply spackling compound.

For wide cracks, use a can opener to scrape plaster from the rear of the edge, making it wider at its bottom than on the surface. This will help to hold the patching compound more securely. Clean out the crack and vacuum or dust it with an old paintbrush.

2 Use a spray bottle to moisten the interior of the crack and pack joint compound or thinset into the recess with a wide putty knife or drywall knife. Press the compound into the recessed edges. When you have filled the crack, draw the putty knife across the surface to smooth it. Allow the compound to dry and reapply if necessary. Sand any rough or high spots smooth with medium-grit sandpaper.

Repairing large damaged areas in plaster

1 Outline a rectangle larger than the damaged area and score the line with a utility knife. Use a wide cold chisel to remove the plaster, working from the scored line to the center. Work in small sections; tap gently to avoid cracking the remaining wall. Measure the thickness of the plaster at the edge of the cutout area and, if necessary, attach ¼-inch plywood strips to the lath (as shown above) so that a ¼-inch drywall patch will be flush with the surface.

2 Cut a drywall patch to the dimensions of the cutout and apply a ¼-inch bead of construction adhesive to the shims or lath. Press the patch into the area. Starting at the corners, drive 1-inch drywall screws around the perimeter of the patch. Space the remaining screws about 6 inches apart. Tape the joints with fiber mesh drywall tape and spread a thin, level coat of drywall compound or thin set over the tape. Sand level when dry if needed.

WHAT IF ...
The wall is sound but not flat or plumb?

Fill minor depressions with thinset. Mark the perimeter of the depression carefully with a carpenter's pencil and apply the thinset with a mason's trowel. When dry, recheck the area with a level or straightedge.

Out-of-plumb walls will be more noticeable at corners. Apply a skimcoat of thinset along the corner to bring adjacent surfaces plumb.

If depressions or out-of-plumb conditions are severe, don't install tile, or remove and replace the wall before tiling.

STANLEY PRO TIP

Level the countertop

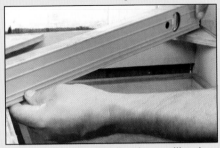

Even if you're tiling a wall and not retiling the countertop, now is a good time to check to see if the countertop is level. If the countertop is not level where it meets the wall, you'll have tapered cut tiles in your wall layout.

Check the countertop with a 4-foot level. If needed, remove the countertop and bring it to level by shimming it along the cabinet top *(page 68)*. Severe problems may require resetting the cabinets.

Removing water-damaged drywall

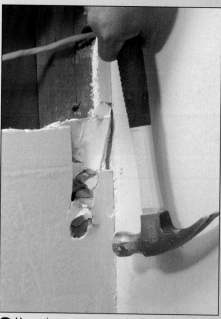

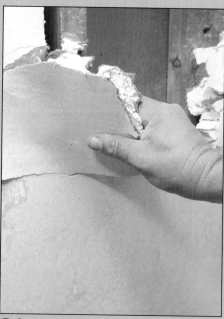

1 Mark the perimeter of the area to be removed. (If the surface is tiled, remove tiles along the edges.) To avoid damaging the surface that will remain, use a utility knife to score the cut line. Cut through the drywall with the knife or drywall saw. Protect the area below with heavy paper.

2 Use a hammer to punch a hole in the drywall between the studs. (If the surface is tiled, it may help to shatter one or two tiles in the center of the wall first.) Enlarge the hole until you can get your hand or a pry bar in it.

3 Grab an edge of the hole you have made and pull off the drywall. To remove large sections, space your hands as far apart as possible. Use a pry bar if necessary. To avoid puncturing the waterproofing membrane when it is installed, pull remaining nails. Check for rot and mold.

STANLEY PRO TIP: **Shore up rotted studs**

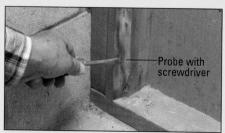
Probe with screwdriver

Scrape rotted areas

Nail new 2×4 stud

Rot decomposes materials through the action of bacteria, and these organisms thrive in wet conditions. Materials that get wet and don't receive enough air to dry them, especially materials behind kitchen and bathroom walls around sinks, tubs, and showers, are especially prone to rot. Rotted wood will not properly support the wall, tiled or otherwise.

Once you have removed the wall covering down to the studs, look for wood with dark blemishes, especially where the stud meets

the bottom plate. Use a screwdriver to probe these joints and those where the stud is fastened to the top plate (left).

If the screwdriver penetrates the wood without much pressure or if the wood feels soft and spongy, you have rot. Dark or splotched areas that are firm are probably not rotted, but may be infested with mold *(page 65)*.

First scrape out the rotted areas with a putty knife (center). Then cut a new 2×4 stud to the same length as the existing stud and toenail it

(drive the nails at an angle through the face) to the top and bottom plate next to the rotted stud (right). Start with a corner stud and work your way along the wall, cutting and adding new boards one at a time.

Extensive rot in the bottom plate or in walls located behind bathtubs may require more complicated repair. Consult a professional carpenter or contractor before proceeding with your tiling project.

Removing water-damaged plaster

1 Outline the perimeter of the area to be removed. To avoid damaging the surface that will remain, use a saw equipped with a diamond or masonry cutting blade to cut through the plaster on the outline. Protect the area below with heavy paper.

2 With a hammer and cold chisel, chip out a hole in the plaster large enough to allow insertion of a pry bar. Push a pry bar as far as you can between the plaster and lath and pry off the plaster in chunks. Remove any remaining nails to avoid puncturing any waterproofing membrane and check for rot and mold.

Stopping mold

Mold is a fungus that lives on the surface of damp materials. Mold does not present much of a threat to the integrity of building materials, but it has an offensive odor and its spores may present a health hazard.

Wear a respirator and clean off moldy surfaces. Then spray liberally with a 50/50 mixture of household bleach and water.

Backerboard is better
Replace drywall in wet areas with backerboard, even if the wall is in good repair.

WATERPROOFING MEMBRANES
Installing membranes

Walls behind a shower enclosure and along a tub need to be protected from water that can migrate and damage the materials behind it. Such walls need waterproofing membranes.

If the condition of the wall has required removal, staple 15-pound felt paper to the studs. Overlap top pieces on lower pieces. Seal the overlaps and staples with asphalt mastic.

If the greenboard is not deteriorated, spread asphalt mastic over it with a ⅛-inch V-notched trowel (page 78). Embed the membrane in the mastic and staple it. Always remove drywall in wet areas.

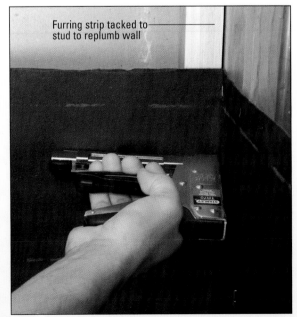

Furring strip tacked to stud to replumb wall

REMOVING COUNTERTOPS

Although you may find many reasons for tiling over an existing laminate, wood, or ceramic tile countertop, removing the existing countertop and building a new base is generally the wiser option.

Removing a laminate or wood countertop is not difficult or time-consuming. Removing existing ceramic tile can add time to your project, but making a new base provides you with the assurance that the job will be done correctly.

One of the main advantages of this option is that you will not raise the height of the countertop. That may not sound like much, but the addition of even the thickness of a new tile surface can disrupt the efficient and comfortable use of the kitchen. In addition, making a new base eliminates the necessity of piecing in numerous cut tiles over the existing backsplash.

Whether you leave the sink in or out of the counter when removing it is a matter of personal choice. Removing the sink, of course, reduces the weight.

PRESTART CHECKLIST

☐ **TIME**
From 45 minutes to one hour after appliances are removed, 2 to 3 times as long if removing tile. Total time will vary with the length and configuration of the countertop.

☐ **TOOLS**
Removing countertop—wrenches, channel-joint pliers, cordless drill and bits, utility knife, pry bar, hammer Removing tile—hammer, cold chisel

☐ **SKILLS**
Removing nuts with wrench, scoring with utility knife, prying, breaking tile with cold chisel, driving screws

☐ **PREP**
Remove appliances

Removing a laminate countertop

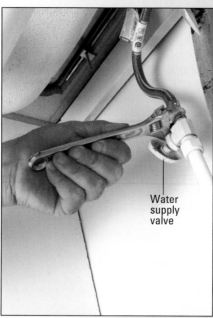

Water supply valve

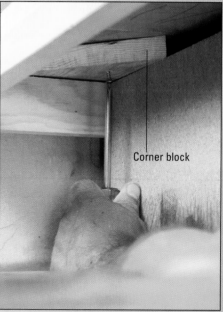

Corner block

1 Turn off the supply valves to the sink and dishwasher and disconnect the lines. Remove the dishwasher *(page 42).* Remove other appliances; **shut off the gas and power** as needed *(page 43).* You can remove the sink or leave it in.

2 Locate corner blocks or cleats that fasten the countertop to the cabinet. Using a screwdriver or cordless drill, unscrew the fasteners. Do not unscrew the fasteners that attach corner blocks to the cabinet frame.

Removing a synthetic resin countertop

Synthetic resin countertops are fastened to the cabinet frame with glue. To remove them, use a sharp utility knife to cut the glue line at the joint between the countertop and the cabinet. Tap a pry bar into the joint and pop the countertop free. If you experience difficulty in inserting the pry bar, tap a thin putty knife along the joint to further loosen the glue bond.

WHAT IF ...
Existing countertop is tiled?

With a cold chisel and hammer, break the center of one tile. Tap the tile with a quick, sharp blow to break it. Chip out the pieces until you have access to a joint. Tap the blade of a wide cold chisel under the adjoining tiles and pop them loose. After removing one or two tiles, you can tell whether the countertop is set on backerboard or in a mortar bed. If the tile is set on backerboard, remove the tile and backerboard on the entire countertop. Hire a pro to saw out a mortar-bed installation.

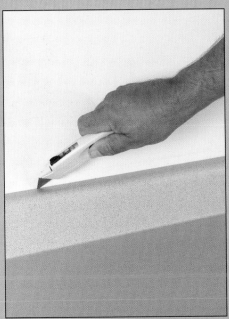

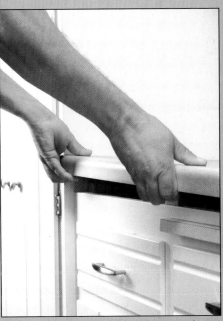

3 To avoid pulling the paint off the wall when you remove the countertop, score the joint between the backsplash and the wall with a sharp utility knife. If the joint is caulked, cut completely through the caulk, if possible.

4 Using a utility knife, score the joint between the countertop and cabinet to break the bond of any glue or caulk. Keep the blade of the knife as perpendicular to the cabinet frame as possible to avoid cutting the wood.

5 Pry off any trim at the countertop edge. Force a pry bar between the countertop and cabinet and pry up the countertop. If the countertop is too heavy to lift, cut it into sections with a reciprocating saw. Saw carefully to avoid cutting the cabinet frame.

REMOVING THE SINK
Removing a countertop sink

1 If the weight of a sink makes removing the countertop difficult, remove the sink first. Shut off the water; disconnect the supply lines and drain pipe. Loosen any retaining screws and remove the clips.

2 Cut any caulk along the edge of the sink with a utility knife.

3 Either push up on the sink from below so you can lift it out, or insert a wide putty knife under the edge of the sink and pry it up until you can grasp it with your hands. Lift the sink up and out of the countertop.

Removing faucets on countertop

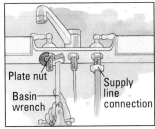

Plate nut

Basin wrench

Supply line connection

Almost all faucets have some style of plate fastened from below with nuts. In most installations, you will not have enough room to maneuver a wrench to loosen the nuts. A basin wrench is specially designed to work in the narrow space between the cabinet and the sink. Remove the supply line connections first, then remove the plate nuts.

Installing a New Countertop Base

Ceramic tile requires a rigid base—use ¾-inch exterior grade plywood. This grade is constructed with moisture-resistant glues. Most lumber outlets will stock 4×8-foot sheets. Larger sheets may be available by special order.

If your countertop spans an open area of more than 3 feet, screw 1× cleats into the front and back frame and attach 1×3 braces. Add bracing under any joints, for example, where two sheets meet in an L-shaped countertop.

Cut the plywood precisely—a 24-inch depth is standard, plus enough to overhang the door fronts by ½ to ¾ inch. If the back wall is not perfectly flat, cut the sheet wide enough to allow you to contour it to the wall. If you're installing a drop-in range, cut the hole for it as you would a sink.

Prestart Checklist

☐ **Time**
About 30 minutes to measure and cut countertop base, 1 to 2 hours to install it, depending on its size and configuration.

☐ **Tools**
Carpenter's level, table saw, hammer, cordless drill and bit, jigsaw and plywood-cutting blade, hole saw

☐ **Skills**
Measuring and leveling, driving fasteners, sawing with jigsaw and table saw (optional)

☐ **Prep**
Remove old countertop, order new sink and faucets

☐ **Materials**
¾-inch exterior plywood, wood shims, 2-inch coated screws, sink and faucet template or stiff cardboard for making template

Checking cabinets for level

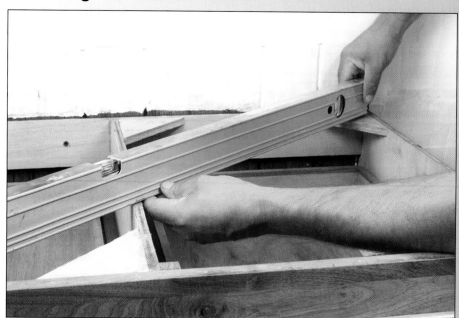

Although an out-of-level countertop will not affect the actual installation of the tile, it will create unattractive tapered edges at the backsplash. Before installing a new countertop, check the cabinet frame carefully to make sure it's level. Set a 4-foot carpenter's level along the rear cabinet edge. Raise the carpenter's level if necessary and mark the wall for level. Next check the sides of the cabinet frame and then both sides of an L-shape counter. If you are installing new cabinets, you can level them by placing shims under the frame. If not, leave the cabinets in place and level the countertop base.

Countertop Base
Use shims to correct for an out-of-level cabinet

Shims

If the results of your checking indicate the cabinet frame is not level, you can add shims to correct the problem instead of removing the cabinets and leveling them.

Cut the countertop base to the correct dimensions and set it in place on the cabinet. Do not anchor it at this time. Place a 4-foot level against the rear of the plywood at the wall and insert shims under the countertop base at locations that will level it. Mark the wall at the locations of the shims. Repeat the process for the sides and the front of the cabinets, being careful not to dislodge shims already in place. Recheck the countertop for level before installing the new plywood base.

Install the new base as noted above, driving the screws through the plywood and the shims into the cabinet frame.

Building a new countertop base

Measure the outside of the cabinet and cut a piece of ¾-inch exterior-grade plywood wide enough to overhang the door fronts by ½ to ¾ inch. Set the plywood on the cabinet and fasten it with 2-inch predrilled screws.

Cutting the sink hole

1 If available, use the manufacturer's template to mark the sink cutout. Otherwise set the sink upside down on the plywood base and trace its outline. Remove the sink and draw parallel lines about 1 inch (or equal to the width of the lip of the sink) inside the outline.

2 Drill a starter hole and cut the interior line with a jigsaw. Keep the base plate of the saw flat on the plywood base and push the saw into the wood slowly. As you cut the final turn, have a helper support the cutout from below to keep the saw blade from binding.

New tile can raise dishwasher

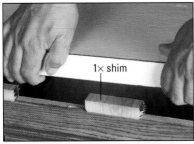

1× shim

The combined thickness of new floor tile and backerboard may raise the dishwasher and other appliances too high to fit under an old countertop. Notching the countertop edge to make the appliance fit creates an unattractive gap and weakens the structure. Instead of cutting, remove the sink and take up the countertop (carefully if you will reuse it). Install shims on the cabinet edge to raise the counter height; reinstall the old countertop or build a new one.

Cutting faucet holes

Some sinks, especially decorator models, require faucets mounted in the countertop (deck-mounted faucets).

If the faucet manufacturer has provided a template for marking the faucet holes, position the template at the appropriate location to the sink hole and use a center punch (a nail or nail set will work also) to mark the points at which to drill.

If a template is not available, you can make one from stiff cardboard, punching out holes and tracing the outline of the faucet plate.

If the faucets have individual spouts, mark the countertop base for each faucet, spacing them at the appropriate location and at an equal distance from the center of the sink basin hole.

Use a hole saw with a diameter equal to the faucet mounts to drill the faucet holes.

Mastering Basic Installation Techniques

Not too long ago setting tile was a job beyond the skills and abilities of most homeowners. In those days tile was set in a thick mortar bed and had to be soaked in water overnight before being set. With the introduction of thinset adhesives and cement backerboard, tile installation moved well within the reach of any do-it-yourselfer.

The techniques of setting tile are easy to learn. If you are starting a tile project for the first time, practice each of the steps before applying it to your floor, wall, or countertop.

Create a practice station by screwing down a couple of pieces of backerboard on a plywood sheet. Mix and spread a small amount of mortar, set the tile, cut a few tiles for the edges in your mock-up, and then grout and clean it. If your practice results don't satisfy you, pull up the installation or start a new one and try again. The individual steps are not complicated, but nothing can substitute for practice before starting a project.

A day's work

In any installation you can lay the cut tiles before the field tiles or vice versa. In general you'll discover that it's easier to lay the field tiles and come back the next day to lay the cut tiles on the edges. That way you won't have to walk on freshly laid tile and risk dislodging it, you can measure the edges precisely and cut tiles to fit. You will also save money on renting tools by limiting all the cutting to one day.

If your tool box does not include tile-installation tools, purchase the best quality you can afford. Most of the tools are not expensive. Don't scrimp on quality, especially that of a carpenter's level and cordless drill. These tools have many uses around the house, and you'll use them for years to come.

Gather all tools and materials ahead of time, think through the installation steps before you start, and take your time.

Most of the techniques presented in this chapter are shown as they are applied to a floor surface, with exceptions for other surfaces noted.

Tile installation is a series of repetitive steps—your skills will improve quickly as a project proceeds.

Chapter Preview

Installing new backerboard
page 72

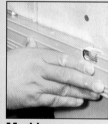

Marking layout lines
page 76

Installing tile
page 78

Cutting tile
page 82

Sort tile for consistency in dye lots or to spread colors of hand-made tile across surface of the room.

Layout lines snapped on surface to be tiled

Cover cracks in slabs with isolation membrane.

Stack tiles close to sections in which you will lay them.

Grouting, caulking, sealing
page 84

Quick-and-easy tile projects
page 86

STANLEY PRO TIP

Snapping a chalk line

To snap a chalk line accurately, the line must be held tightly on the surface. Pull the line from its housing. Place the metal tab at one end of the surface and the housing at the other. Keeping the line tight, reach out as far from the housing as you can, lift the line about 4 inches off the surface and let it snap back.

You may be able to hook the metal tab in the perimeter recess of a slab or wood floor. If you can't, snapping the line is a two-person task, one holding the tab and the other holding the housing.

INSTALLING NEW BACKERBOARD

Because backerboard should be installed with its edges centered on joists and studs, mark the joist and stud locations before you start. Since you won't be able to see marks after you have troweled on the thinset, mark joist locations on the wall and stud locations on the ceiling.

Offset the joints where the sheets meet by half a sheet, where possible. Leave at least a ⅛-inch gap between sheets (use an 8d nail), and a ¼-inch gap at the walls (about the size of a pencil).

It's easier to scoop thinset out of the bucket with a margin trowel; then spread it with the notched trowel recommended by the adhesive manufacturer.

PRESTART CHECKLIST

☐ **TIME**
About 30 to 45 minutes per square foot of surface

☐ **TOOLS**
Cutting backerboard—drywall square, carbide scriber, utility knife, rasp
Cutting holes—tape measure, cordless drill, carbide hole saw, compass, utility knife, and hammer for large holes
Installing backerboard—mason's trowel, margin trowel, corner drywall knife, cordless drill, utility knife

☐ **SKILLS**
Precise measuring and cutting, driving fasteners with cordless drill, troweling

☐ **PREP**
Prepare, vacuum, and damp-clean surfaces. Install waterproofing membrane in wet locations. Cut and install new countertop base.

☐ **MATERIALS**
Installing backerboard—thinset, backerboard, 1¼" and 2" backerboard screws, 2" gummed fiber mesh tape, 2×4 lumber for bridging (walls only), 8d nails

Cutting backerboard

1 If you are not finishing the floor, protect it with a tarp. Backerboard particles will easily scratch a floor. Mark the line to be cut and position a drywall square or metal T-square on the line. Using a carbide backerboard scriber and firm pressure, scribe the cut line. Make several passes.

2 Stand the sheet on edge or turn the sheet over; working from the side opposite the scored line, snap the board.

Cutting small holes

1 Set the board against the pipe or other obstruction. Mark the diameter of the hole to be cut. Use a tape measure to locate the center of the hole. For faucets, measure the location of each faucet hole from the wall and from the tub or floor.

2 Use a cordless drill and carbide-tipped hole saw or coring saw to cut small holes in backerboard. Place the drill point of the saw on your mark; use light pressure and high speed to cut through.

3 Using a utility knife, and keeping the pieces at an angle, cut through the board to separate the two pieces. Depending on how deeply you made your first cut, you may have to make several passes with the knife to separate the pieces.

4 Backerboard cuts are rough, whether made with a carbide scriber or a utility knife. Pieces being joined should have as smooth an edge as possible. Use a contour plane with a serrated blade, a rasp, or a masonry stone to smooth out the edge. Keep the tool perpendicular to the edge of the board and pass over it several times until its surface it flat.

Cutting large holes

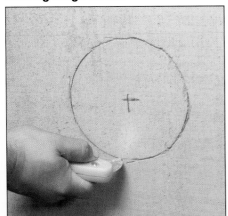

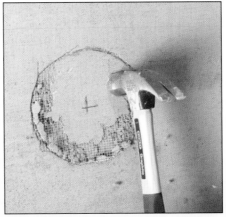

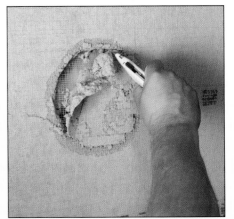

1 When the diameter of a hole to be cut exceeds the size of available hole saws, measure the obstruction and use a compass to mark its location on the backerboard. Then score completely through the backerboard mesh with a utility knife or carbide scriber.

2 Support the cutout with the palm of one hand, if necessary, and tap the scored edge with a hammer. Continue tapping until the surface around the circumference crumbles. Alternatively, drill a series of small holes around the circumference.

3 Using a utility knife, cut through the mesh on the opposite side of the board. Push the cutout through and smooth the edges with a rasp, serrated contour plane, or masonry stone.

Installing backerboard on floors

1 Mix and pour thinset *(page 78)*. Hold the smooth side of a notched trowel at a 30-degree angle and spread the mortar in a thick, even coat, forcing it into the subfloor. Then, keeping the notched side of the trowel in contact with the floor and at a 45- to 75-degree angle, work the mortar into ridges.

2 While the mortar is still wet, tip the board on a long edge and hinge it toward the floor. Line the first board on a joist and keep a gap of ⅛ inch between boards, ¼ inch at walls. Manufacturer's directions may vary, but never butt one board against another. Walk on the board to set it in the mortar.

3 Using a cordless drill and phillips bit, drive backerboard screws through the board and into the subfloor at about 8-inch intervals. Use 2-inch backerboard screws at the joists and 1¼-inch screws in the field. Set the screws so they are flush with the surface of the board.

Installing backerboard on walls

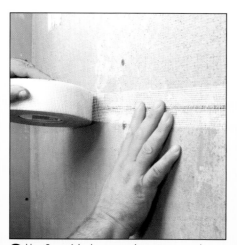

1 If necessary, nail blocking between studs to support joints. Apply construction adhesive to the studs. Screw the board to the studs and blocking. Rest the next pieces on ⅛-inch spacers (8d nails) before fastening.

2 Use 2- or 4-inch gummed tape over each backerboard joint. Press the tape into the joint and unroll it as you go. Use a utility knife to cut the tape at the end of the joint.

3 Apply a thin coat of thinset mortar to the taped joint with a margin trowel. Trowel on enough mortar to fill the joint and level it with the backerboard. Feather the edges smooth.

4 Apply 2-inch pregummed fiberglass mesh tape over each joint, pressing the tape firmly on the backerboard. The tape cuts easily with a utility knife. Use 4-inch tape (if available) for increased strength. Alternatively, you can imbed ungummed tape in a thin coat of mortar applied to the joints. Use this method where stronger joints are required—in stone-tile installations, for example.

5 Whether you have used ungummed or pregummed tape, finish the joint by applying a thin coat of thinset mortar over the tape. Use a margin trowel to scoop mortar from the bucket and apply it so that it levels the recess in the joint from side to side. Feather the edges to avoid creating high spots under the tiled surface.

Taping corners

Tape corners with either 2-inch or 4-inch gummed fiberglass mesh tape. In either case, do not precut the tape to length. Unroll it as you press it into the joint and cut it when you reach the end. Precut lengths of gummed tape may roll up and stick to themselves before you get them on the board.

If using 2-inch tape, place one length along one edge and another length along the other edge. Bridge the central edges of the corner with a third length of tape. Four-inch tape makes the job progress more quickly. Fold the tape in half as you press it into the corner.

If using ungummed tape, first spread a thin coat of mortar into the corner joint and smooth it with a drywall corner knife. Then imbed the tape in the mortar. With any kind of tape, finish the joint with a thin coat of mortar feathering the edges smoothly.

STANLEY PRO TIP

Backerboard screw snaps

Backerboard fasteners, unlike drywall screws, are made to withstand the rigors of tile installations. Occasionally, however, one will snap off. Check the torque setting of your cordless drill to make sure the clutch slips when the screw just dimples the board. If a backerboard screw snaps, remove the loose piece and drive another about 1 inch away from the first one.

MARKING LAYOUT LINES

Perhaps no other task requires more precision than marking reference and layout lines. These lines keep your tile square to the room and evenly spaced.

Mark reference lines perpendicular to each other. Save time setting tiles by locating these lines where a grout joint will fall when you install the tile. You can use your layout sketch to find this point, but it's better to dry-lay and space at least one row of the actual tiles in both directions. Mark the edge of the tile, then snap the lines.

Next mark layout lines to establish grids for laying tiles in sections. How many you use depends on how complicated your layout is, how quickly the adhesive sets up (its working time), your skill level (if you're less skilled, use more lines), and the size of the tile (larger tile will generally mean fewer lines). Establish a grid with which you feel comfortable (about 2-foot squares are a good size to start). Measure from the reference lines in both directions by an amount that equals several tiles (plus grout joints) and snap lines at these points.

PRESTART CHECKLIST

☐ **TIME**
About 5 minutes to measure and snap each line, more if dry-laying tile to establish lines

☐ **TOOLS**
Laying out floors—tape measure, chalk line
Laying out walls—tape measure, 4-foot level, chalk line

☐ **SKILLS**
Reading a spirit level, measuring accurately

☐ **PREP**
Surface preparation, installation of backerboard

☐ **MATERIALS**
Layout sketch, loose tile, and spacers

Marking layout lines on floors

1 Using your layout sketch *(page 31)*, mark the floor several feet from one wall where a grout joint will fall. To double check your layout, dry-lay and space the tiles along each axis. Mark the ends of this line at both walls.

2 Snap a chalk line at the points you have marked. Repeat the process between the other walls. Use the 3-4-5 triangle method *(page 32)* to square the lines. Measure from each of these reference lines distances equal to an even number of tiles and joints and snap layout lines at these points.

LAYOUT IS COMPLICATED
Snap additional layout lines

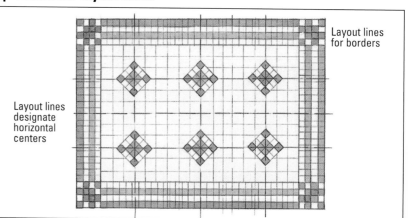

Layout lines for borders

Layout lines designate horizontal centers

Layout becomes more complicated with decorative tiles and borders. Although you can lay such decorative items by eye, installing the tile will go more quickly and the result will be much more attractive if you snap additional layout lines.

Once you have snapped the major layout grids on the floor or wall, measure and mark the position of decorative tiles or borders. Snap a line on both axes at each point the pattern or the tile size changes.

Marking layout lines on walls

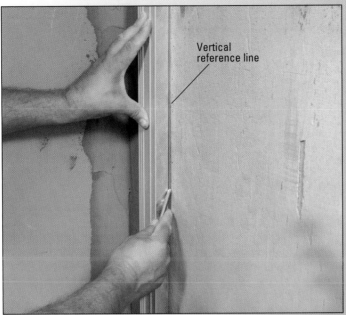

Vertical reference line

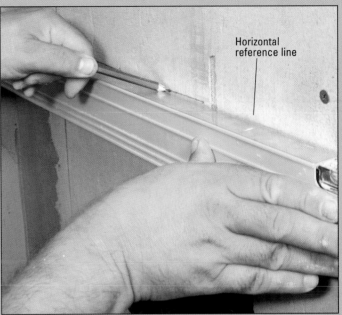

Horizontal reference line

1 Hold a 4-foot carpenter's level vertically on the wall and at least 2 feet from a corner, preferably on a plane where a grout line will fall. Adjust the level until the spirit bubble indicates it is straight up and down. Taking care not to disturb the level, trace a penciled line down its edge. Extend the line to the floor and ceiling by snapping a chalkline over the one you have marked.

2 Position the level horizontally on the chalk line, about midway up the wall, and preferably on a plane where a grout joint will fall. Adjust the level until the bubble is centered in the glass and scribe a line along the level. Extend this line with a chalk line. You don't have to check the intersection for square with the 3-4-5 triangle method.

From each line, mark the wall at intervals that correspond to an equal number of tiles (include the grout joints) and snap layout lines.

STANLEY PRO TIP

Protect layout lines on the floor

Chalk layout lines on the floor can easily be erased or blurred as you walk and work in the room. To protect them, spray each of the lines with an inexpensive hair spray. Purchase a spray with a heavy hold. Apply a fairly thick coat, but not enough to obscure the lines. The spray dries almost immediately, will not wear off, and won't interfere with the adhesive bond.

Where to start?

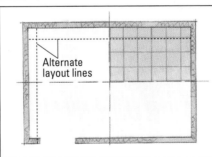

Alternate layout lines

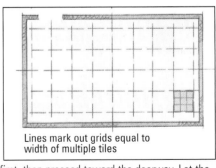

Lines mark out grids equal to width of multiple tiles

Snapping layout lines in grids will help you lay the room in manageable sections and keep each section straight. Although there is no rule that governs how many grids to snap, one rule will keep you from tiling yourself into a corner—always start your project at a location away from a doorway.

You may be able to get by in a small room with only one pair of lines, although grids are recommended. Lay the field tiles in the corner first, then proceed toward the doorway. Let the mortar dry for a day and then come back and lay the cut tile on the edges.

Large rooms will likely require more grids than small rooms. They also tend to lend themselves to quadrant installations. Set out the tile and lay it in the quadrant most removed from the doorway. Then go back and set the adjacent quadrant, the corner quadrant, and finally the section that exits to the door.

INSTALLING TILE

Prepare the surface using the methods described on *pages 39*. Slab floors and drywall and plaster in nonwet areas may not require the installation of backerboard. Install backerboard on wood surfaces and walls in areas that will get wet, such as bathrooms or entryways.

Before you trowel on the mortar, figure out how many tiles you need in each layout grid and stack them around the room close to each section. That way you won't have to go back and forth to supply yourself with fresh tiles when you start laying each grid.

Sort through all of the tile boxes to make sure the dye lots match and separate out any chipped tiles. Use these for cut pieces.

If you are installing saltillo or handmade tile, its color may be consistent within each carton but may vary from box to box. Sort through the tiles; at each layout grid, mix some from each box. Mixing will spread the colors evenly in the room and keep them from occurring in patches.

PRESTART CHECKLIST

☐ **TIME**
About an hour to trowel and set 4 to 6 square feet (varies with tile size)

☐ **TOOLS**
½-inch electric drill, mortar mixing paddle, notched trowel, 4-foot level, utility knife, beater block, hammer or rubber mallet

☐ **SKILLS**
Mixing with power drill, troweling

☐ **PREP**
Install backerboard, clean surface, and snap layout lines

☐ **MATERIALS**
5-gallon bucket, thinset, spacers, ¾-inch plywood squares

Setting the tile

1 Pour the water in a bucket, then add about half the thinset. Mix the thinset with a ½-inch drill and a paddle designed for mortar. Keep the speed below 300 rpm and the paddle in the mix to avoid adding air. Add thinset a little at a time. Let the mix set for 10 minutes before applying.

2 Pour enough mortar to cover a layout grid. Holding the straight edge of the trowel at about a 30-degree angle, spread the mortar evenly, about as thick as the depth of a trowel notch. Spread the mortar to the layout line; comb it with the notched edge at about a 45- to 75-degree angle.

Mix the thinset

Whether you have chosen thinset or organic mastic, bring it into the room to acclimate it to normal room temperatures—ideally between 65° and 75° F. Mix thinset with water that is clean enough to drink and clean out the bucket after each mix; mortar and adhesive residue can cause your new batch to begin curing prematurely.

Adding the powder to the water a little at a time reduces airborne mortar dust and makes mixing easier. Let the mixture set for 10 minutes so that the water will penetrate any remaining lumps. Then mix again to remove lumps. To test the consistency, load a trowel with mortar and hold it upside down. If the mortar falls off the trowel easily, add more dry powder and remix. Thinset should be about as thick as peanut butter. Clean the bed before troweling.

STANLEY PRO TIP

Choosing the right trowel

The size of the the notches in the trowel you use will depend on the thickness of the tile. The depth of the notch and therefore the ridge it forms in the adhesive should be about two-thirds the tile thickness.

Use ¹⁄₁₆- to ⅛-inch V-notched trowels for thin tiles, such as glazed wall tiles. For 6- to 8-inch floor tiles, use a ¼- to ⅜-inch square-notched trowel, and for large tiles (more than 12 inches), use a deep (½-inch) square-notched trowel.

Combing adhesive so it forms the right-sized ridges requires that you hold the trowel at about a 30-degree angle and keep the edges of the trowel in constant contact with the substrate. If you have trouble making ¼-inch ridges with a ¼-inch trowel, switch to a ⅜-inch notch and hold the trowel more perpendicular to the surface.

3 Set the first full tile at the intersection of your layout lines, positioning it with a slight twist as you embed it in the mortar. Do not slide the tile in place—sliding can reduce the thickness of the thinset and build up mortar between the joints. Keep the edges of the tile on the layout lines.

4 Using the layout order you have chosen *(page 102),* lay the next tile in place with the same twisting motion, keeping the tile aligned on your layout line. Insert spacers between the tiles and adjust the tiles to fit.

5 Continue laying tiles along both legs of the layout lines (for a jack-on-jack design, as shown above, see *page 102)* or in the order of your design, spacing the tiles as you go.

Testing the mixture

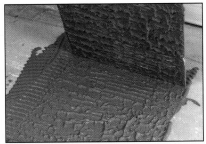

Properly applied thinset will form ridges that compress to cover the entire back of the tile when it is embedded. If thinset is applied too wet, it will not hold these ridges. A dry thinset application will not compress and will result in the tile adhering to the top of the ridges only.

Test your thinset mixture by pulling up a tile and examining the back. If the thinset completely covers the surface, the mixture is correct, as shown above.

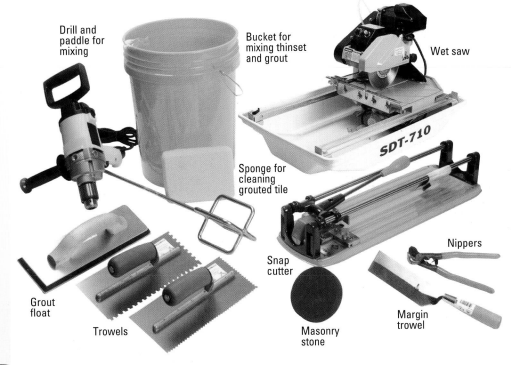

Drill and paddle for mixing

Bucket for mixing thinset and grout

Wet saw

Sponge for cleaning grouted tile

Snap cutter

Nippers

Grout float

Trowels

Masonry stone

Margin trowel

Setting the tile (continued)

6 Periodically check to make sure the tile conforms to the layout lines in both directions. Lay a long metal straightedge or 4-foot level on the edge of the tile. This edge should align itself with the layout lines. Each joint within the pattern should also be straight. Scrape off any excess thinset that may have spread over a layout line. Adjust the tiles to straighten the joints, if necessary.

7 Continue laying the tiles according to your chosen pattern, spacing and checking them as you go. Don't kneel or walk on set tiles. If you need to straighten a tile that is out of reach, lay down a 2-foot square of ¾-inch plywood to distribute your weight evenly and to avoid disturbing the tile. Cut at least two pieces of plywood to use, so you can position one while kneeling on the other.

Setting spacers

When laying loose tiles (not sheet-mounted), use plastic spacers to keep the tiles the proper width apart.

Insert spacers vertically in the joint after you set each successive tile. That way the tile will move into the correct placement after it is embedded in the mortar. Once you reach a point where tiles form corners, flip the spacer down into the corner. Pull the spacers before grouting, even if the manufacturer's instructions indicate that you can leave them in place. Spacers may show through the grout.

Working with mosaic tile

Mosaic sheets require special care when you are setting them. Their numerous edges can tip within the sheet or rise higher than the adjoining sheet. To keep them flat, gently tap them level with a grout float, both within the field of the sheet and at the edges. Use this same technique when aligning them to the contour of a drain recess on a shower floor.

Leveling the tile

1 When you have finished laying one section or grid of tile, place a long metal straightedge or a 4-foot carpenter's level on the surface and check for any tiles that are higher or lower than the overall surface. Make a beater block out of a 12- to 15-inch 2×4 covered with scrap carpet. Tap high tiles in place using the beater block and hammer.

2 If you discover tiles that are lower than the rest, pry them up with the point of a utility knife and spread additional adhesive on the back of the tile. Set the tile back in place and level it with the beater block. Clean excess mortar from the joints while the mortar is still wet. Run the blade of a utility knife in the joint, flicking out the excess as it accumulates on the blade. Pick up loose bits of mortar with a damp sponge. Let the thinset cure at least overnight.

WHAT IF ...
The tiles have uneven edges?

Tiles with irregular edges, such as saltillo and handmade pavers, may be difficult to keep straight, and spacers will not align the uneven edges. To keep such tiles aligned, make your layout grids small—a nine-tile (three-by-three) layout works well.

Trowel adhesive one grid at a time and set the tiles in place. Adjust the tiles until the appearance of the joints is consistent and expect to make a few compromises.

Setting stone tiles

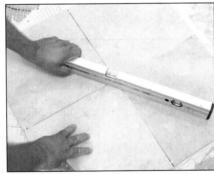

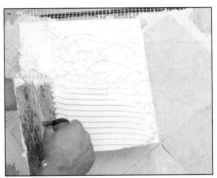

When setting marble or translucent stone, use white thinset; colored mortar may show through. Marble, granite, and travertine tiles look best with thin 1/16-inch grout joints. Slate looks best with wider joints, up to 1/2 inch.

Stone tiles are more brittle than ceramic tile and therefore more prone to cracking. Make sure the setting bed is stable and flat. Damp-

sponge any dust off the back of the tiles, if necessary. Apply the mortar recommended by the distributor or manufacturer of the stone.

Check each tile for level with a straightedge (above, left), pulling up and back-buttering tiles that are low (above, right). Make sure the edges of one tile are not higher than another.

CUTTING TILE

Cutting tile requires a little skill and patience—save yourself installation time by practicing a few cuts first.

If the cut tiles in your project will be the same width, cut all of them at once, trowel on the adhesive, and lay the tiles. If the tiles will not be uniform, cut each one separately. Do not let adhesive set longer than its working time while you're making the cuts.

Tile cutting is accomplished with a variety of tools. For only one or two cuts, you need only a tile nipper or a rod saw with a carbide blade.

A snap cutter makes quick work of cutting thin tile, such as most wall tiles. Rent a wet saw to cut thicker tiles. Do not cut quarry tile with nonslip carbide chips in the surface. The chips will quickly dull the blade. If you have several tiles to cut, the wet saw may prove well worth its cost.

Wet-saw blades are cooled by water, either from an outlet that flows water on the blade or from water in a trough below it. Do not cut tile without the water in place.

Cut tile edges are rough. Either hide them under toekicks or smooth them with a masonry stone.

Sizing the cut

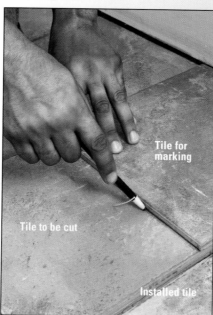

Straight cut: Place the tile to be cut flush to the wall or obstruction, lined up on top of an installed tile. Place another tile over the tile to be cut, with its edge against the wall. Trace the edge with a marker. Draw the cutting line parallel to the mark but shorter by the width of two grout lines.

L-shape cut: Place the tile to be trimmed first on one corner and then the other, marking the cut lines with a full tile as you would for a single straight cut. Cut each side shorter than the mark by the width of two grout lines.

PRESTART CHECKLIST

☐ **TIME**
Less than five minutes to mark and cut each tile

☐ **TOOLS**
Felt-tip or china marker, tri-square, snap cutter, wet saw, masonry stone, tile nippers

☐ **SKILLS**
Measuring and marking tile precisely, cutting tile with nippers, snap cutter or power saw

☐ **PREP**
Install backerboard and field tile

☐ **MATERIALS**
Tile

STANLEY PRO TIP

Don't wash away the line

The blade of a wet saw is cooled with water, which will wash away a cut line made with a felt-tip marker. When marking tiles that will be cut with a wet saw, use a china marker so the line won't wash away.

SAFETY FIRST
Protect your eyes when cutting

Cutting tile with a snap cutter is not especially dangerous, but you should wear eye protection to guard against any fine chips, especially from glazed tile.

A wet saw can discharge chips and larger pieces of tile at high speed, so eye protection is a must. Wear ear protection to guard against damage from the noise of the saw.

Wear safety glasses when cutting tile with nippers, too.

Save on rental costs
Cut all your edge tiles in one day. That way you pay only one day's rental for a wet saw.

Making straight cuts

Scoring wheel

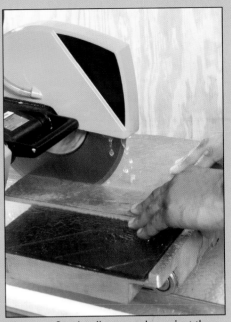

Curved cuts: Set the tile to be cut against the obstruction, lining up its edges with tile already laid. Mark the width of the cut by setting a tape measure on each edge of the obstruction. Move the tile to one side of the obstruction and use the tape to mark the depth of the cut.

Snap cutter: Insert the tile in the cutter, aligning the scoring wheel on the cut line. Pull or push the scoring wheel across the cut line, using firm pressure throughout the stroke. Score the tile in one pass. Hold the tile firmly in place and strike the handle with the heel of your hand.

Wet saw: Set the tile securely against the fence with the cut line at the blade. Turn on the saw and feed the tile into the blade with light pressure. Increase the pressure as the saw cuts the tile and ease off as the blade approaches the rear of the cut. Keep the tile on the table at all times.

Making curved cuts

1 Using a wet saw, make several relief cuts from the edge of the tile to the curved cut line. Relief cuts do not have to be exactly parallel to each other, but make sure they stop just short of the curved line.

2 Place the jaws of tile nippers about an inch away from the curved line and carefully snap out the waste at the relief cuts.

3 Working the nippers on the cut line, snap away the remaining excess. Don't try to "bite" through the tile with the nippers. Instead, grasp the tile tightly with the tool and use a prying motion.

GROUTING, CAULKING, AND SEALING

Grouting, caulking, and sealing are not difficult tasks, but they do take time. Don't rush these activities—they affect both the final appearance of your tiling project and its longevity.

Bring all materials into the room to acclimate them to its temperature, preferably between 65° and 75°F. Prepare the surface by removing spacers and cleaning excess mortar from the joints and surface. Lightly mist the edges of nonvitreous tile with water so they won't take too much moisture from the grout. Vitreous tiles do not require misting.

Use a margin trowel to mix grout in clean containers, following manufacturer's instructions, adding powder to liquid a little at a time. Let it set for 10 minutes and restir it to loosen its texture. Grout should be wet enough to spread, but not runny.

PRESTART CHECKLIST

☐ **TIME**
From 15 to 30 minutes to mix, float, and clean a 4-foot-square section (varies with tile size). About five minutes to caulk a 10-foot joint, 45 minutes to seal a 15×20-foot floor, longer if applying sealer to joints only.

☐ **TOOLS**
Utility knife or grout knife, grout float, nylon scrubber, margin trowel, grout bag (optional), applicator or mop for sealer, caulk gun

☐ **SKILLS**
Spreading grout with float; using caulk gun

☐ **PREP**
Install all tile and let mortar cure

☐ **MATERIALS**
Grout, bucket and water, rags, sponge, sealer, caulk

Grouting tile

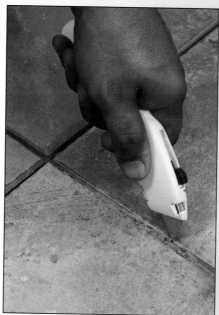

1 Remove spacers if you have not done so already. Inspect the joints for any remaining adhesive and scrape it out with a utility knife or grout knife. Remove any remaining hardened mortar from the tile surface with a nylon (not metal) scrubber.

2 Mix the grout to the consistency recommended by the manufacturer; dump or scoop a small pile out with a margin trowel. Working in 10-square-foot sections, pack the grout into the joints with a grout float. Hold the float at about a 30- to 45-degree angle; work it in both directions.

WHAT IF ...
The grout joints are wide?

Irregular tiles look best with wide grout joints, but wide joints may be hard to fill with a grout float. Use a grout bag for these tiles and for rough tile whose surfaces will be difficult to clean.

Fit a metal spout on the bag equal to the width of the joint. Fill the bag with grout. Working down the length of a joint, squeeze the bag, overfilling the joint slightly. Compact the excess and sweep loose grout with a stiff broom when dry.

STANLEY PRO TIP

Avoid voids when mixing grout

Power mixing can introduce air bubbles in gout and leave voids in it. Mix grout by hand with a margin trowel, adding the powder to the water. Let the mix set for 10 minutes, then remix before applying.

Tips for grouting stone

Use the grout recommended by the manufacturer. Nonsanded grout tends to recede when curing, and you may need to apply this kind of grout twice if the joints in your stone installation are set at $1/16$ inch. Stone should be sealed before grouting to ease cleaning.

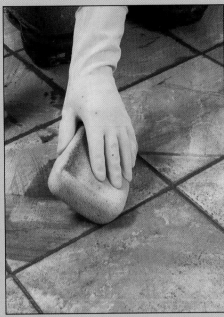

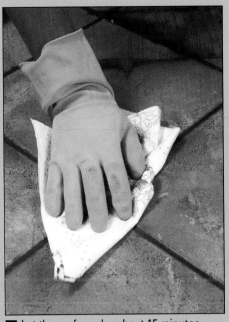

3 Once you have grouted a section, hold the float almost perpendicular to the tile and scrape the excess off the tile surface. Work the float diagonally to the joints to avoid lifting the grout. If you remove grout, replace it in the joint and reclean the surface. Let the grout set.

4 When a just-damp sponge won't lift grout from the joint, you can start cleaning. Wring out all excess water from a damp sponge and rub the surface in a circular motion. Rinse and wring out the sponge often. Repeat parallel to the joints to make them neat, and once more to finish cleaning.

5 Let the surface dry about 15 minutes and then remove the grout haze from the surface with a dry, clean rag. Avoid terry cloth material; it might lift out uncured grout. Tile with a matte finish may require another cleaning with fresh water and a clean sponge.

Sealing tiles

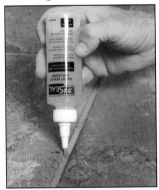

Although latex or polymer-modified grouts will resist staining, you'll get the best protection from stains by sealing the grout.

On glazed and other impervious tiles, apply the sealer only to the

joint using an applicator designed for this purpose.

To protect saltillo and other soft-bodied tiles, seal the entire surface with a mop or applicator as recommended by the manufacturer.

Caulking the joints

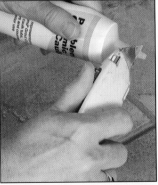

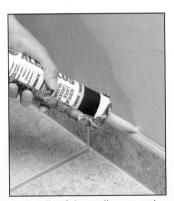

Use a utility knife to cut the nozzle to the width of the joint and at a 45-degree angle. Cut through the nozzle in one pass. Before you apply the caulk, you may want to practice the techniques on scrap.

Starting in one corner, squeeze

the handle of the caulk gun gently and apply the caulk to the joint. Keep the caulk gun moving as you squeeze so the caulk won't overrun the joint. Finish the surface of the caulk with a wet finger or sponge. Light pressure will avoid gouging.

QUICK-AND-EASY TILE PROJECTS

Before you engage in a full-scale floor, wall, or countertop, you may want to practice on one of these simple projects. Whatever project you begin, make sure that the surfaces are flat, clean, and dry before setting the tile.

Installing a tile top can add new life to an old table. The existing top may be somewhat warped, so you may want to install small-sized tile which does not crack as easily as large tile. Slight variations in the table surface may add to its charm. If the table is severely warped, try sanding it with a belt sander first. The tabletop installation shown here uses thinset for the adhesive. If the table is primarily decorative and won't receive heavy use, you can use organic mastic as the adhesive.

PRESTART CHECKLIST

☐ **TIME**
About one hour to tile a small table, slightly more if edge tiles are cut; 30 minutes for each stair riser; 15 to 20 minutes for tiled house numbers

☐ **TOOLS**
Tabletop tiles—chalkline, framing square, utility knife, margin and notched trowels, masonry stone
Stair risers—margin trowel, utility knife
House numbers—margin trowel, square

☐ **SKILLS**
Snapping precise layout lines, troweling mortar, and laying tiles

☐ **PREP**
Clean surfaces

☐ **MATERIALS**
Tile, thinset or mastic, grout, rags, duct tape

Tiling a tabletop

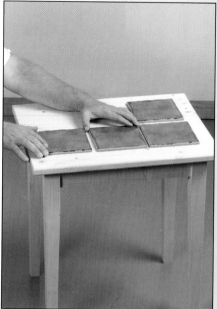

1 Lay one course of tiles "dry" (without thinset) on the table across its width and another course spanning its length. Adjust the courses to leave at least a half tile at the edges, if possible. Mark the ends of the table at the edges of each row.

2 Remove the dry-laid tile; snap reference lines at the marks on the table. Test the intersection of the lines with the 3-4-5 triangle method *(page 32)* or a framing square. Adjust the line if necessary to make them perpendicular to each other. Snap additional layout grids, if necessary.

Tiling stairway risers

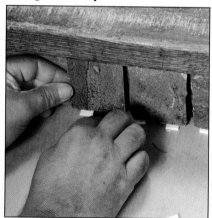

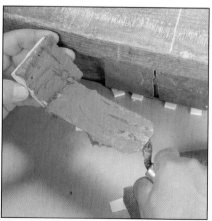

1 It is not necessary to avoid cut tiles on stair risers, but the installation will be easier if you purchase tiles that will cover the riser evenly. Set out the tiles to mark any tiles that must be cut.

2 Back-butter each tile with thinset, about two-thirds the thickness of the tile. Press the tile against the riser. Tape the tiles to hold them till the mortar cures. Grout if using thinset and if appropriate to the tile.

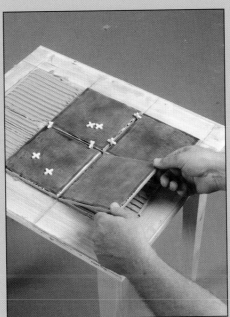

3 Mix enough thinset to cover the table (or a section of it) and pour the mortar on the table. Spread it to an even thickness with the straight edge of a trowel, keeping it along the layout lines. Then use the notched edge to comb the mortar to create ridges.

4 Starting at the intersection of a layout grid, lay the field tiles in the pattern of your choice, keeping them on the layout lines and spacing them as you go. Remove excess mortar from joints and let the mortar set up. Measure and cut any edge tiles, rounding the cut edge with a masonry stone.

5 When the mortar is dry, set the edge tiles with the factory edge to the outside of the table. Let the mortar cure and force grout into the joints with a grout float. Let the grout set up and scrape the excess off with the float. Clean the tiles at least twice and remove the haze with a soft rag.

Applying tiled house numbers

1 Set the numbers on a flat surface, spacing them to allow for any joints. Measure the dimensions of the layout. Using a square, mark the outline on the outside house wall.

2 On siding, use organic mastic to anchor the tiles. Use thinset on masonry surfaces. In both cases, back-butter the tiles and press them firmly on the surface.

3 As soon as you have applied each tile, tape it in place with duct tape. Let the adhesive cure for at least 12 hours, then remove the tape.

TILING FLOORS, WALLS & COUNTERTOPS

Once the preparation steps are complete, you'll find setting tile less tedious and more rewarding. As the tiles are laid, you'll begin seeing the results of all your planning.

If you have several tile projects planned, start with the least complicated or the smallest. That way you can build your skills and gain experience. Refer to the previous chapters at any point you need more information.

Mixing mortar and thinset

Before you begin to mix adhesives, read the manufacturer's directions carefully. Always mix mortar and grout in a clean container. Any residue in the bucket may cause the material to cure prematurely. Clean buckets and utensils after each mixing to save time and avoid problems.

Carefully heed the "working" time—how long it takes the material to set up. Once the setting up has started, tile will not adhere. Grout that has exceeded its working time will not work properly into the joints and will pop out when dry. If either material has begun to set up before you are finished working with it, scrape it off the surface, remix, and reapply.

At first you might need a little practice to discover how much of each material will cover an area before it sets up. Installation of large tiles will go more quickly than small tiles. Start with a small batch and work up to larger areas as your skills increase.

Heat and humidity will affect mortar and grout. You may need to mix a wetter consistency in hot or dry conditions. However, do not add water to mortar that has begun to set up in the heat; you will weaken its strength. Discard the mixture and start over.

Working with mastics

Mastic ingredients may settle in the can, leaving an oily-looking liquid on top. Stir it until the consistency is smooth.

If you open a can of mastic stored for a long time and it has begun to harden, throw it out and purchase fresh stock.

Application techniques remain essentially the same no matter what surface you're tiling.

CHAPTER PREVIEW

Tiling a small entryway
page 90

Tiling floors
page 92

Tiling walls
page 98

Hold the grout float at a 45-degree angle when forcing grout into joints.

Set and grout the countertop tile before beginning the backsplash.

Use a dampened sponge to smooth grout and clean excess off tiles.

Tiling a countertop and backsplash can be planned as a single project or as separate projects. Backsplashes can be hard to reach and the work can go slowly; work in small sections to avoid the grout setting up before you're finished.

Tiling a shower enclosure or tub surround
page 101

Tiling a kitchen countertop and backsplash
page 104

TILING A SMALL ENTRYWAY

A small entryway is a good beginning tile project, requiring a straightforward application of basic skills. An entryway opens to many rooms; lay it out so it looks best from its most-viewed perspective.

PRESTART CHECKLIST

☐ **TIME**
About 30 to 45 minutes per square yard to prepare floor and set tile

☐ **TOOLS**
4-foot level, small sledge and cold chisel, right-angled grinder or belt sander (for wood floor), tape measure, chalk line, margin trowel, roller, notched trowel, straightedge, carbide scriber, utility knife, snap cutter or wet saw, nippers, masonry stone, grout knife, caulk gun, grout float, hammer, cordless drill, putty knife

☐ **SKILLS**
Troweling, snapping with chalk line, setting tile, grouting with float

☐ **PREP**
Repair structural defects

☐ **MATERIALS**
Bucket, thinset, isolation membrane, tile, spacers, caulk, grout, rags, sponge, water, threshold and fasteners, backerboard and tape (for wood floor), foam backer rod

Tiling an entry slab

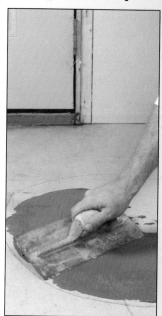

1 Examine the entryway slab for high spots, depressions, cracks, and other defects. Work in sections with a 4-foot level and mark the defects. Fill depressions, level high spots, and roughen slick surfaces.

2 "Bandage" each crack in the slab with an isolation membrane. Apply the adhesive with a roller, let it cure (follow the manufacturer's directions), and cover the adhesive with the membrane *(page 59)*.

3 Dry-lay tiles to test your layout, keeping small cut tiles to a minimum. Then snap a reference and as many layout lines as the pattern needs *(page 76)*. Start at the door and trowel on thinset *(page 78)*.

LAYOUT LINES
Measure and make square

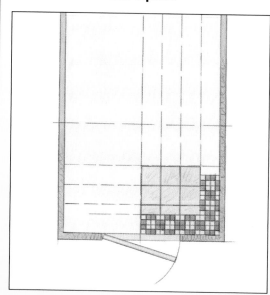

Snap perpendicular reference lines either at the midpoint of the walls or at least 2 feet from them. Snap the line at a point over which a grout joint will fall in the installation. Use the 3-4-5 triangle method to adjust the lines, if necessary, to form a right angle at the intersection *(page 32)*.

Measure from the reference lines (not from the wall) to locate the start of any border tiles. If you measure from the wall, you may be thrown off by discrepancies in the surface and transmit them to your layout.

Establish layout grids by measuring in each direction a distance equal to the width of several tiles and grout joints. Snap layout grids at these points. Double check the marks before you snap so the grids will be the same size and square.

4 Set field tile first on the layout lines. Insert spacers as you go and check the sections with a straightedge to make certain they're straight. Clean excess mortar from the joints with a utility knife.

5 When the mortar under the field tiles is dry, cut and set the edge tile *(page 82)*. Round the cut edges with a masonry stone to give them a finished appearance. Clean the joints and caulk the joint at the wall.

6 Let the edge tiles cure before you grout. Force grout into the joint with a grout float and, when it's set slightly, scrape the excess off the surface. Clean the grout from the surface and wipe off the haze with rags.

7 If your threshold didn't require installation before the tile, install it now. Cut the threshold to fit the doorway, if necessary, and install it with fasteners recommended by the manufacturer.

Tiling an entry on a wood subfloor

Shore up the joists and the subfloor if necessary *(page 57)* and prepare the surface with the same methods used on a slab. Mix enough thinset to allow you to use it within its working time (the time it takes to "skin" over) and trowel it on the floor, smoothing first with the straight edge of a trowel and combing it with the notched edge.

Screw down cement backerboard with the edges centered on the joists, offsetting subsequent joints and spacing the edges ⅛ inch apart. Drive screws in the backerboard on the edges and within the field.

Tape the backerboard joints with 2-inch pregummed tape and spread a thin coat of thinset over the tape.

Don't forget the expansion joint

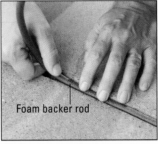

Foam backer rod

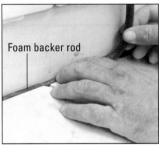

Foam backer rod

Tile floors expand and contract with changes in temperature. Expansion joints cushion the expansion of tile against the wall and keep the tile from cracking.

An expansion joint is a gap filled with a compressible material and topped off with caulk. Foam backer rod is available in a variety of thicknesses. Purchase backer rod that fits snugly *(page 27)*.

On a slab, insert foam backer rod into any control joints in the field of the slab and also along the perimeter at the wall. Push the backer rod in place with a wide putty knife.

On a tiled wood floor, insert the backer rod in the ¼-inch gap between the cement backerboard and the wall. Finish the joint with caulk colored to match the grout.

TILING FLOORS

Ceramic tile is the most stable finished floor covering, but it's best to acclimate it to the room before setting it. Bring tile and other materials into the room at least a day in advance.

Sort tiles for consistent coloring and according to design or texture patterns. Stack tiles around the room near the sections in which you'll lay them, counting out enough to fill each section. Organizing your materials will reduce trips to another room to get more tiles.

If you haven't done so already, verify the accuracy of your dimensioned layout plan by setting a row of tiles in each direction in a dry run on the floor.

You can leave outswinging doors in place. Remove inswinging doors as needed.

PRESTART CHECKLIST

☐ **TIME**
About 30 to 45 minutes per square yard to prepare and set tile

☐ **TOOLS**
4-foot level, small sledge and cold chisel, right-angled grinder (slab) or belt sander (wood floor), chalk line, margin trowel, notched trowel, straightedge, utility knife, carbide scriber, snap cutter or wet saw, nippers, masonry stone, grout knife, caulk gun, grout float, hammer, cordless drill, putty knife, tape measure

☐ **SKILLS**
Power sanding, snapping chalk lines, driving fasteners, troweling, laying tile, grouting

☐ **PREP**
Repair structural defects

☐ **MATERIALS**
Bucket, thinset, isolation membrane, roller, tile, spacers, caulk, grout, rags, sponge, water, backerboard, screws, tape, foam backer rod, tile base or bullnose, threshold and fasteners

DIMENSIONAL KITCHEN DRAWING

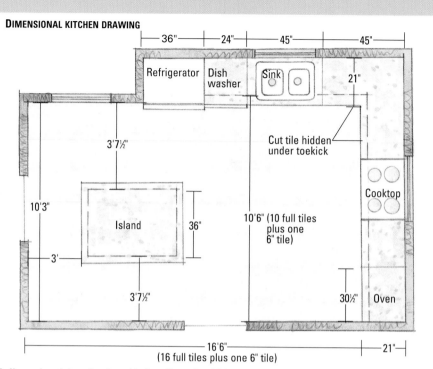

A dimensional drawing for a kitchen floor should include spaces currently housing appliances. When you note dimensions on the plan, add the thickness of any baseboard that will be removed. Measure up to the edge of toekicks under the cabinets.

DIMENSIONAL BATHROOM DRAWING

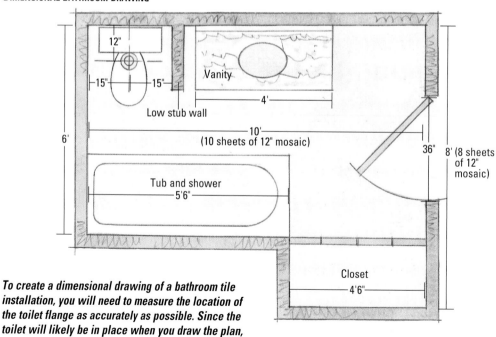

To create a dimensional drawing of a bathroom tile installation, you will need to measure the location of the toilet flange as accurately as possible. Since the toilet will likely be in place when you draw the plan, you will not be able to see the flange. Estimate its location by measuring from the side wall to half the width of the toilet base and from the back wall to about one-fourth of its length.

A. Installing backerboard

1 Examine the floor carefully and mark defects—high spots, indentations and depressions, popped nails, and cracks. Fix all defects that could interfere with the adhesive, backerboard, or tile installation. Install a waterproofing membrane over the floor if necessary.

2 Mark joist locations on the walls and measure from a parallel wall to the joists. Cut the board so the edges will be centered on the joists. Starting on a wall away from the door, trowel a section of thinset, lay the board, and fasten with screws. Continue the process, working toward the doorway.

3 Starting again at a wall away from the door, tape each backerboard joint with 2-inch pregummed mesh tape. Use 4-inch tape at the corners if the backerboard goes up the wall. Trowel a thin coat of thinset over the tape.

FIX ALL DEFECTS
Level high and low spots

Work in sections and use a 4-foot level. Place the level on the floor and rotate it within a section, noting and marking defects with a carpenter's pencil.

Although the floor shown here is a wood floor *(page 56)*, the techniques for fixing defects on a slab are essentially the same

(page 58). First chip out and fill major cracks. Then pour self-leveling compound or trowel thinset into depressions and feather the edges level with the floor. Use a belt sander to remove high spots on a wood floor; use a right-angled grinder with a carbide abrasive wheel on a slab. Dewax surfaces and clean.

WHAT IF . . .
I need a waterproof membrane?

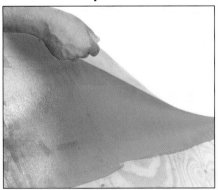

In wet areas such as bathroom floors, apply adhesive with a roller, then the membrane, then trowel on more adhesive *(page 57)*. Working in sections, start on a wall away from a door and cover the entire floor. Make sure the adhesive is spread all the way to the edge of the floor.

B. Marking layout lines

1 Use your dimensioned drawing to guide the placement of layout lines. From the midpoint of the walls or at a distance equal to several tiles and grout joints, mark the location of the lines where a grout joint will fall. Dry-lay tiles and spacers in both directions to locate the line precisely. Anchor one end of the chalkline or have a helper hold it and snap the lines. Adjust the first pair so they are perpendicular and snap lines in layout grids of a manageable size.

2 If you have designed a border or accent pattern on your dimensioned drawing, snap layout lines where the field tile ends and the border begins. Mark lines within the pattern where the tile changes shape or size. If the design is especially complicated, dry-lay the tiles on a piece of heavy cardboard, trace and cut out the pattern, and use the cardboard as a stencil to lightly spray-paint the pattern on the floor. Tape the stencil down.

LAYOUT LINES
How to lay out different room configurations

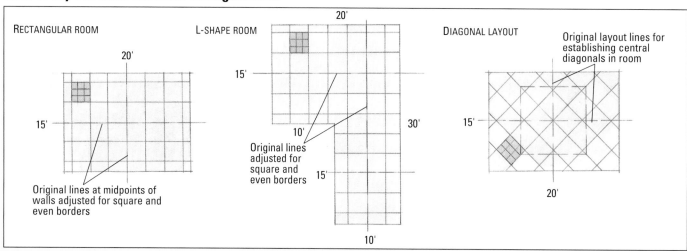

RECTANGULAR ROOM

20'

15'

Original lines at midpoints of walls adjusted for square and even borders

L-SHAPE ROOM

20'

15'

10'

30'

15'

10'

Original lines adjusted for square and even borders

DIAGONAL LAYOUT

15'

20'

Original layout lines for establishing central diagonals in room

Different room configurations can alter your approach to layout lines and grids. For small square or rectangular rooms, the number of lines will be minimal and you will probably not need a line at the edges to mark the location of cut tiles. In a large room with large handmade pavers (above left) add lines marking the location of the edge tiles and snap 3-foot grids to help keep things straight. In an L-shape room, make sure to position the lines along the longest walls so they fall in both sections. In all cases snap the first pair of reference lines where a grout line will fall.

C. Laying the tiles

1 Mix enough thinset for the number of layout grids you will set at one time. Dump mortar in the first grid, spread it to the lines, and comb it. Lay the first tile in a corner of the grid, twisting it slightly as you embed it. Continue laying tile, inserting spacers as you go. Check each grid with a straightedge to make sure the joints are properly aligned. Clean excess thinset from the joints and surface. Cut tile for the edges and around obstructions and set it.

2 When the mortar has cured (usually overnight), mix enough grout to cover a section and apply it with a grout float *(page 84–85)*. Let the grout set up until a damp sponge won't pull it from the joint, then scrape the excess off the tile surface with the float. Damp-sponge the residue from the surface, smoothing out the joints. Damp-sponge again. Let the surface dry. Scrub the haze from the surface with a rag. Grout the next section. Caulk the perimeter joint.

Hide the edges

On most tile, cut edges will look noticeably different from the molded factory edge. You can smooth the edges of cut tile with a masonry stone to make them appear less conspicuous, but smoothing takes time. Where possible, hide the cut edges of the tile under the cabinet toekicks, setting the tile with its factory edge toward the field tile.

CUT TILE
Working around pipes and flanges

Cutting tile to accommodate pipes and flanges is easier, and you can make more precise cuts after the field tile has been laid *(page 83)*.

Set the tile to be cut on the field tile, with the cut edge against the pipe or flange. Make an allowance for the size of the grout joint. You can mark the width of the cut by eye or hold a small square against the pipe. Mark the dimensions of the cut with a felt-tip pen or china marker. Then mark the tile slightly wider

than these lines, so the cut will allow for any expansion of the pipe.

If the arc of the cut is shallow, you can nibble it out with a tile nippers. If not, use a wet saw to cut relief cuts from the edge to the arc. Remove the relief cuts with a tile nippers and bite out the remaining material to the arc. Remove just a little material at a time. Trying to nip out too much may crack the tile.

D. Adding a tile base

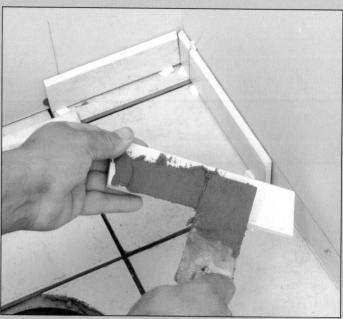

1 Out-of-level floors force you to adjust the base tiles to make their top edges level. You'll make up the difference in the joint at the floor. Lay the bullnose tile against the wall with spacers. Adjust the tile heights with plastic wedges until the top edges of all tiles are level. Make sure the joint at the floor is as even as possible from one end to the other. Continue the layout on adjacent walls. Mark the wall at the top edge of the final layout.

2 Remove the tiles and snap a level chalkline at the mark you made. Mark all the walls with chalklines in a similar fashion. Mix up enough thinset to cover the area in which you'll be working. Back-butter each tile and set it in place.

STANLEY PRO TIP

Installing transitions

Most tiled floors require a threshold of some kind to bridge the difference in height from the tile to an adjacent floor. Wood thresholds present a professionally finished appearance. Cut the threshold to the dimensions of the doorway and trim its width to fit between the edge of the tile and the flooring below. Nail it in place with ringshank nails. Set the nailheads and fill the holes with matching wood filler.

WHAT IF . . .
Bullnose is not available for your tile?

If bullnose trim is not available in the style of your tile, cut trim tile from the same stock you laid on the floor. Determine the height of the edging you want and cut enough tiles to run the entire length of the wall. Cut each piece of tile only once. Even if you can get more than one piece from a large floor tile, you'll want a factory edge on top. Install the cut tile and grout the top edge if the factory edge is not finished to your liking.

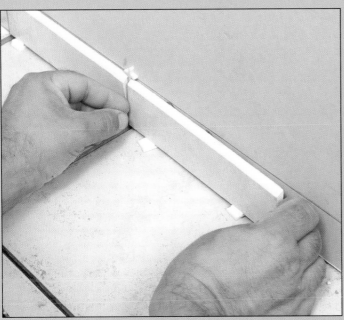

3 Press tile in place, inserting spacers. Use the plastic wedges to keep the top edge in line. About every 3 feet, use a 4-foot level to make sure the top edge is level. Adjust the tile if necessary by gently pushing or pulling on the wedges. Gently remove excess mortar from the joints with a utility knife and clean the surface. Set and clean corner tiles and let the mortar cure overnight before grouting.

4 As a final step, grout the trim tiles and caulk the joints at the floor and top edge. Force grout into the vertical joints with a grout float. When the grout has partially cured, remove the excess from the joint at the floor with a utility knife and from the surface with a damp sponge. Sponge-clean the surface at least twice and wipe off the haze with a clean rag. Caulk the joint at the floor and along the top edge of the trim. Smooth the caulk with a wet finger or sponge.

Trimming doors

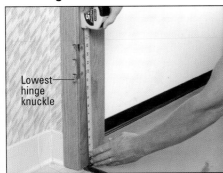

Lowest hinge knuckle

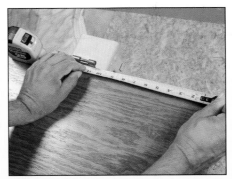

1 Remove the door if necessary. Tap the hinge pin with an 8d nail and pull the pin out with pliers. You may have to tap out a stubborn pin with a hammer and straight screwdriver inserted under the head of the pin.

Measure the distance from the tiled floor to the bottom of the lowest hinge knuckle on the door jamb.

2 Subtract ¼ inch from your measurement and, using this length, measure from the top of the lower pin knuckle on the door to the bottom of the door. Mark the door at this point; using a carpenter's square and a straightedge, extend the line across the bottom of the door. Transfer the line to the other side of the door.

3 Score the lines on both sides of the door with a utility knife. Use a straightedge to keep the knife on line and score deeply with several passes.

Clamp the door securely to a solid worktable and clamp a guide that will keep the saw blade on the cut line. Trim the excess off the door, sand the edges smooth, and rehang the door.

TILING WALLS

Establishing layout lines on walls is much easier than on a floor. Hold the level on the wall in both a vertical and horizontal plane, and when the bubble centers in the glass, trace intersecting lines.

Unlike floor tiles, which tend to stay in place, wall tiles are affected by gravity and tend to slide down the wall. Organic mastic is one solution—tile sticks to it almost immediately. Mastic is not as strong as thinset mortar, however, and not as water resistant. You can keep tile in place on thinset by using spacers, nails, or tape.

If you are tiling a wall and a floor, tile the floor first so you can continue the grout joints up the wall in the same pattern as the floor. Install a cove base, then start wall tile at the cove base. If you are tiling adjacent walls, set the back wall first. Tapered edges on a side wall are less visible.

PRESTART CHECKLIST

☐ **TIME**
About 30 to 45 minutes per square yard to prepare and set tile

☐ **TOOLS**
Wide putty knife, 4-foot level, sanding block, small sledge and cold chisel, stud finder, tape measure, chalkline, utility knife, carbide scriber, margin trowel, notched trowel, straightedge, cordless drill, grout knife, snap cutter or wet saw, nippers, masonry stone, caulk gun, grout float

☐ **SKILLS**
Reading spirit level, troweling, laying tile, grouting

☐ **PREP**
Repair structural defects

☐ **MATERIALS**
Deglossing agent, release agent, bucket, thinset, dimensioned lumber for battens, backerboard, screws, tape, tile, spacers, caulk, grout, rags, sponge, water, tile base or bullnose, nylon wedges

A. Laying the tile

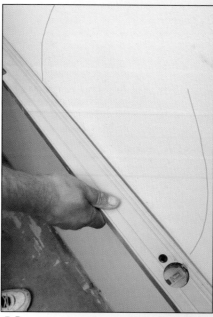

1 Remove any wall covering and degloss paint. Using a 4-foot level, examine the wall in sections, marking high spots, depressions, and other defects that would interfere with the tile. Pay close attention to corners to check for plumb *(page 63)*.

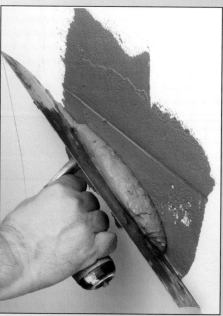

2 Skim-coat a layer of thinset on any walls that are out of plumb and fill depressions. If installing backerboards on studs, mark stud centers on the ceiling. Cut and fasten backerboard, centering its edges on the studs. Position the backerboard pieces to minimize cutting and waste.

WHAT IF ...
There's a window on the wall?

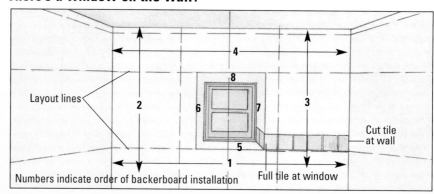

Layout lines

Numbers indicate order of backerboard installation

Cut tile at wall

Full tile at window

Windows add complications to wall layouts. If possible, arrange the pattern with a full tile around the perimeter of the window and cut tiles at the edges of the wall. You can get this balance fairly easily if the window is centered and if tile covers the surface evenly or leaves at least a ½-tile at the corners.

If a perfectly balanced layout won't work, try adjusting the grout lines or inserting decorative tile. Trim tiles at the window's edge might even out the layout. Install the window tiles first to establish the grout lines for wall field tile; then tile the remainder of the back wall, working upwards.

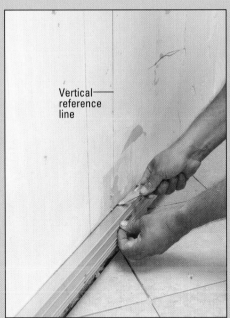

3 Set a 4-foot level vertically on the wall about 2 feet from a corner, over a grout joint. If the wall meets an outside corner, set the level where the inside edge of a bullnose will fall. Pencil a line down the level, extend it to the floor and ceiling. Repeat the process on the horizontal plane.

4 Snap layout grids from the reference lines with additional lines for the edge of border tiles. Mix enough adhesive to cover the sections you can lay within its working time. Work from the bottom up, spreading the adhesive evenly and combing it with the notched edge of the trowel.

5 Starting at the bottom, press field tile into the mortar with a slight twist. Continue laying the pattern of your choice, using spacers if your tile is not lugged. When the field tile is set, cut and install the edge tiles.

Keeping the tiles on the wall

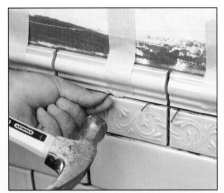

If you're not using a coved base and your layout results in cut tiles at the floor, tack a level 1× or 2× batten along the plane on which your first full tiles will be laid. The batten will keep the rows in place and prevent the tiles from sliding down the wall. Even with a coved base or a batten and spacers, it still may be necessary to take extra precautions to

keep the tile on the wall while the adhesive cures. Drive nails partway into the wall at least every third of each tile's length and tape the tiles with masking tape. If your layout calls for a coved tile base, install it first, leveling it with nylon wedges. Then tile up the wall.

WHAT IF ...
Tiles are lugged (prespaced)?

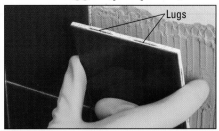

Lugged tiles make spacing on wall installations easy. They come with small bisque lugs raised on the edges and don't require additional spacers to keep them properly aligned.

Because the lugs are fired into the tile at the time of manufacture, they don't allow you to make the grout joints narrower. Determine the actual dimensions of the tile when you purchase it so you know how much space each tile actually covers.

B. Grouting the tile

1 When the adhesive has cured to the manufacturer's specifications, inspect the joints for excess adhesive. Remove any adhesive left in the joints with a utility knife or grout knife and clean any excess off the tile surface. Mix enough grout to cover a section and force it into the joints with a grout float, keeping the float at the proper angle *(page 84)*. Work the float in both directions to fill the joints; work diagonally to remove excess grout.

2 When the grout has cured enough that a damp sponge won't pull it out of the joints, scrape off the excess with the float held almost perpendicular to the surface. Clean the surface and smooth the joints with a damp sponge, then repeat the cleaning with clean water and a clean sponge. When a haze forms, wipe it with a clean rag. You may have to wipe with some pressure to take off the haze.

WHAT IF ...
The wall has electrical outlets on it?

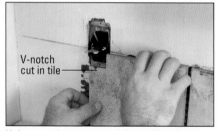

Unless you have removed the wall surface, the thickness of finished surface will extend beyond the edges of electrical outlet boxes. This may cause the receptacle screws to be too short to anchor the receptacle. A box extension will remedy the problem, but if local codes don't require an extension you can fix the problem with longer screws.

First, **turn off the power to the circuit** and remove the cover plate and receptacle screws. Remove one receptacle screw completely so

you can take it to the store to buy a screw ½ inch longer and of the same diameter. Push the receptacle into the box out of your way.

In the top and bottom tiles, cut V-notches (use tile nippers) that line up with the tabs and screw holes on the top and bottom of the box. Spread adhesive to within ¼ inch of the box and embed the tile. When the mortar cures, pull out the receptacle from the box and fasten it with the longer screws inserted through the notches.

Turning an outside corner

Outside corners can present problems, especially if they are not plumb. Hide slightly out-of-plumb situations by skim coating the wall as plumb as you can with thinset. Then overlap bullnose tiles or edge tiles on the full tiles on the other wall. As long as the tiles meet crisply, the out-of-plumb wall may not be as noticeable.

TILING A SHOWER ENCLOSURE OR TUB SURROUND

Because a shower enclosure is a wet installation, the walls and structure must be properly prepared and waterproofed. Use felt paper with cement backerboard, but not with greenboard or waterproofed gypsum board *(page 22)*.

A bathtub introduces additional challenges. If the tub is level, set a full tile at its edge. To minimize the awkward appearance of an out-of-level tub, make the bottom row at least three-fourths of a tile high.

For a shower enclosure, extend the tile and the backerboard at least 6 inches above the showerhead. For a tub surround only, install the backerboard and tile 12 inches above tub. Work quickly to keep the adhesive from skimming over.

PRESTART CHECKLIST

☐ **TIME**
About 20 minutes per square yard to prepare and set tile

☐ **TOOLS**
Utility knife, stapler, hair dryer, 4-foot level, tape measure, chalk line, carbide scriber, margin trowel, notched trowel, straightedge, cordless drill, snap cutter or wet saw, nippers, grout knife, masonry stone, caulk gun, grout float

☐ **SKILLS**
Ability to use hand tools, cordless drill, and trowels

☐ **PREP**
Repair structural defects, remove finished wall material to studs

☐ **MATERIALS**
Asphalt mastic and 15-lb. felt paper, staples, bucket, thinset, dimensioned lumber for battens, backerboard, screws, tape, tile, spacers, caulk, grout, rags, sponge, water, tile base or bullnose, nylon wedges, accessories

A. Installing waterproof membrane and backerboard

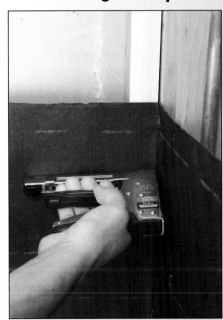

1 Cut felt paper long enough to turn all corners and cover the surface in a single run. Apply asphalt mastic to the studs, then staple the paper, warming it with a hair dryer before pressing it into the corners. Overlap top pieces on lower ones and seal overlaps with asphalt mastic.

2 Cut backerboard so its edges will be centered on the studs and fasten it to the studs with backerboard screws. When fitting backerboard above a tub, leave a ¼-inch gap between the bottom edge of the board and the tub rim.

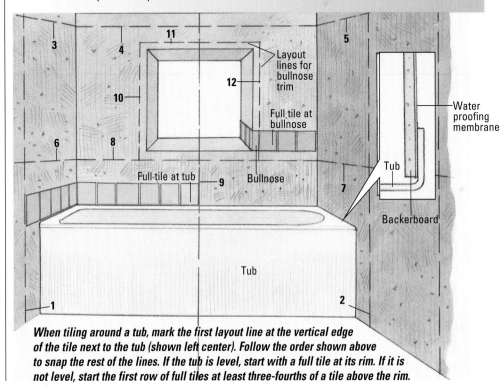

Layout lines for bullnose trim

Full tile at bullnose

Water proofing membrane

Tub

Full tile at tub

Bullnose

Backerboard

Tub

When tiling around a tub, mark the first layout line at the vertical edge of the tile next to the tub (shown left center). Follow the order shown above to snap the rest of the lines. If the tub is level, start with a full tile at its rim. If it is not level, start the first row of full tiles at least three-fourths of a tile above the rim.

B. Installing the tile

1 Using your dimensioned layout drawing, locate the point on which a horizontal and vertical grout line will fall. Hold a 4-foot level on both planes and mark reference lines. Then snap layout grids whose dimensions equal the width of the tiles and grout joints.

2 Tack a batten on the bottom of the wall if necessary *(page 99)* and prepare enough adhesive to cover the number of layout grids you can lay before the adhesive begins to set up. Set field tiles on the back wall first, in the order of your layout pattern. Don't set tiles around fixtures yet.

3 When the back wall is done, set the side walls starting from the front, leaving cut tiles for the back edge at the corner of the adjoining wall. Tape the tiles if necessary to hold them in place *(page 99)*. Remove excess adhesive from the joints; let it cure.

LAYOUT PATTERNS
Patterns determine the order of setting tile.

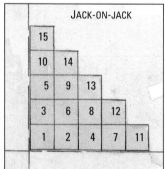

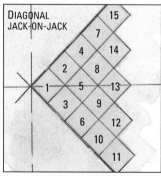

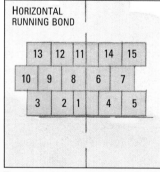

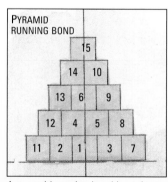

A jack-on-jack pattern is one of the easiest patterns to use. Set the first tile at the intersection of the layout grid or quadrant and lay the remaining tiles in the order shown above. As an alternative, you can set the legs of the quadrant and fill in the interior.

Diagonal patterns always result in cut tiles on the edges. Before choosing a diagonal pattern, work with your dimensioned layout drawing to make sure these edge tiles will be as close to a full diagonal as possible. A border will frame a diagonal pattern nicely.

To make a horizontal running bond work, find the exact center of the first tile and lay it on one axis of your layout lines. Work from that tile to the left and then to the right. Then center the next row on the same axis. Check the alternating grout lines with a straightedge.

A pyramid running bond is perhaps the most difficult to keep straight because it stacks the centers of tiles not only on alternate rows but also on both sides of the vertical axis. Before laying this pattern, mark all the tiles that will be centered on this axis.

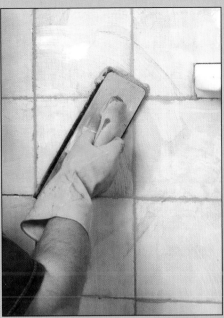

4 When the adhesive has dried overnight, cut and set the edge tiles and remove excess adhesive from the joints. Then mark, cut, and install the tile around the showerhead and faucets. Leave at least ¼ inch around the fixtures and fill the recess with silicone caulk. Let the adhesive cure.

5 When the adhesive is dry, clean the surface and joints of any remaining excess. Mix grout and apply it with a grout float, forcing it into the joints in both planes. Let the grout cure until a damp sponge won't lift it out of the joints.

6 To scrape the excess off the surface, hold the float almost perpendicular to the tile and work diagonally to avoid pulling the grout from the joints. Dampen a sponge, wring it out thoroughly and clean the surface twice, smoothing the joints. Scrub off the haze with a clean rag.

REFRESHER COURSE
Cutting tile

1 To mark a straight cut, line up the tile to be cut exactly on top of a tile already set. Place another full tile over that one, with its edge against the wall or other obstruction. Mark the line with a felt-tip pen or china marker. Mark the cut line parallel to the first, but shorter by the width of two grout lines.

2 Cut thick tiles and large quantities of tile with a wet saw. Set the tile on the fence with the cut line aligned to the blade. Feed the tile into the blade with light pressure. Increase the pressure as the saw cuts the tile; use light pressure as the blade approaches the rear of the cut.

3 Start curved cuts by making relief cuts with a wet saw. Cut from the edge of the tile to the curved line. Place the jaws of the tile nippers about 1/16 to 1/8 inch away from the curved line and carefully snap out the waste at the relief cuts. Working the nippers on the cut line, snap away the remaining excess.

Installing surface-mounted fixtures

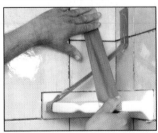

When you set the wall surface, leave a space for surface-mounted accessories, such as soap dishes, cutting the tile around it if necessary. Use a margin trowel to apply mortar to both the recess and the back of the accessory and press the unit into place. Keep it centered with wedges. Tape it in place until the mortar dries, then caulk the joint.

TILING A KITCHEN COUNTERTOP AND BACKSPLASH

A countertop and backsplash can be planned as a single project or as separate projects.

If you are setting a countertop and backsplash, lay the backsplash tiles before the countertop front edge to avoid disturbing the edge tiles when you lean over the counter.

The installation shown on these pages includes a waterproofing membrane, an element you can omit if the counter will be used infrequently or will not be subject to spills associated with food preparation or frequent cleaning. With or without the membrane, use latex or acrylic modified adhesives and grout. Seal the grout joints to protect them from staining.

PRESTART CHECKLIST

☐ **TIME**
About 20 minutes per lineal foot of countertop to prepare and set tile

☐ **TOOLS**
Utility knife, stapler, hair dryer, 4-foot level, tape measure, chalk line, carbide scriber, margin trowel, notched trowel, straightedge, cordless drill, snap cutter or wet saw, nippers, grout knife, masonry stone, caulk gun, grout float

☐ **SKILLS**
Reading a level, troweling, laying tile, grouting

☐ **PREP**
Repair structural defects, remove old countertop and build new countertop base

☐ **MATERIALS**
Asphalt mastic and 15-lb. felt paper, staples, bucket, thinset, backerboard, screws, tape, tile, spacers, caulk, grout, rags, sponge, water, bullnose or V-cap edge tile, nylon wedges, sink

A. Preparing the surface

1 Measure and cut polyethylene sheets or 15-lb. felt paper to the size of the countertop, including the backsplash if desired. Allow enough for the overhang. Staple the sheets to the plywood base.

2 Cut backerboard to fit both sides of the sink. If the sink has reinforcing bars, cut grooves in the pieces to match. Set the sections at both sides of the sink cutout, but do not fasten them. Measure the remaining spaces at the rear and front of the sink and cut and groove backerboard to fit.

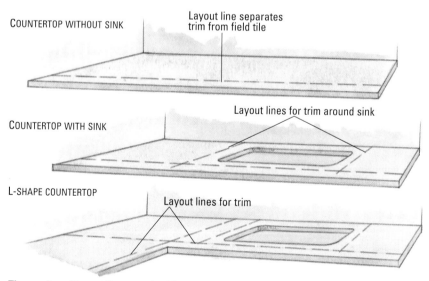

COUNTERTOP WITHOUT SINK

Layout line separates trim from field tile

COUNTERTOP WITH SINK

Layout lines for trim around sink

L-SHAPE COUNTERTOP

Layout lines for trim

The number of layout lines required for a countertop installation varies with its complexity. At a minimum, a counter with no sink needs a line that locates the front edge tile. Counters with a sink require lines for the front edge and the perimeter of the sink. With a tiled backsplash, carry the lines up the wall.

B. Laying the field tile

3 Drop the sink in to make sure that its reinforcing bars fit, then fasten the board to the plywood base with backerboard screws. If using backerboard on the backsplash, back-butter it to make the job easier. Tape all joints and edges and apply a thin coat of thinset over the tape.

Snap reference and layout grids on the countertop and backsplash as necessary to help you keep the layout straight. Be sure to snap a line where the edge tiles will be laid, both on the front of the countertop and around the perimeter of the sink. Dry-lay as many tiles as necessary to make sure the lines are located correctly. Pull up a section of the dry-laid tiles and apply thinset to the section. Install the field tiles first on the entire countertop surface. Clean the grout lines with a utility knife and remove excess mortar from the tile surface. Let the adhesive cure overnight.

Carry grout joints up the wall

If you are tiling a backsplash with the same tile as the countertop, establish your layout lines on the counter at a point on which a grout line will fall. Then carry the lines up the backsplash area so the backsplash joint will match the joints in the top.

If the backsplash tiles are different from countertop tiles, you must lay out the backsplash separately.

Layout lines
You don't have as much working room on a countertop so make your layout lines precise.

WHAT IF ...
Countertop is L-shape?

L-shape countertops require a slightly different approach than rectangular counters.

Snap a layout line on the front of both legs to locate the position of the edge tiles. Make sure that this line extends the full length of each leg. Then snap the remaining lines for the rear edge tile and tile around the sink. Dry-lay the tiles to keep the location accurate.

Begin the installation of the tile at the intersection of the two legs, working first on the leg without the sink. Then, set the field tiles on the second leg, then the backsplash tiles. Clean the joints and the tile surface. Set the V-cap or bullnose edge tiles last to avoid the risk of disturbing them by leaning over the countertop.

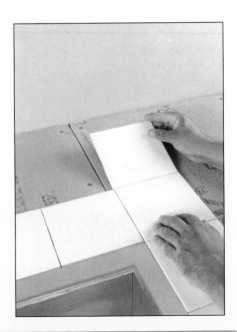

C. Setting the trim tile and grouting

Bullnose edging

1 Measure and cut the trim tile to be set around the sink. If using bullnose tile, cut corners on a wet saw. Dry-fit the corners to make sure the grout line will be the same width as the others. Spread thinset on the backerboard and back-butter each tile so they adhere properly. Let the adhesive cure until it just begins to set up. Carefully remove any excess from the joints and perimeter with a utility knife.

2 If using bullnose tile on the top edges instead of V-cap edging, you can keep the tile in line with a thin batten on the edge of the plywood base. Trowel on thinset and lay the bullnose tile in place on the top of the plywood base. Let the mortar cure, and then remove the batten. Back-butter the front edge tiles with thinset. If necessary, tape the tiles in place until the mortar cures.

STANLEY PRO TIP

Stone countertops

Stone countertops must be level to avoid cracking. Check each section as you lay it. For a high-sheen finish that matches the surface of the tile, you'll want to polish it.

Polishing stone edges and surfaces is a tricky business, and the tools are expensive for a one-time use. Ask your supplier for the name of a professional who can do the job for you.

KEEP THE TILE IN LINE
Working with bullnose or sheet-mounted tiles

Keeping both field and edge tiles lined up properly on a countertop can be difficult if you do not have the room to maneuver a long straight edge.

To help keep bullnose edges in line, cut a strip of wood to the thickness of the front edge tile. Tack this batten to the front of the plywood base flush with the top. Install the bullnose so its front edge is flush with the front of the batten.

Sheet-mounted tiles often will shift as the mesh backing softens in the thinset. To prod them back in line, use the smooth edge of a trowel as a short straightedge.

3 When the mortar is dry, clean any residue, if necessary. Mix the grout thoroughly to remove any trace of lumps. Spread and force it in to the joints with a grout float held at about a 45-degree angle. Make sure all the joints are completely filled.

4 Clean sections as soon as the grout sets up slightly. Remove the grout from the surface before it hardens to avoid scratches. Remove excess grout with the float. Use a wrung-out wet sponge to smooth the joints and remove the excess from the surface. Repeat the cleaning at least once more and wipe off the haze with a rag.

WHAT IF ...
You are using V-cap or wood edge?

If you are trimming the countertop with V-cap, first trowel thinset on the countertop edge. Then back-butter the inside bottom edge and embed the cap in the mortar. V-cap firings often vary a little from field-tile sizes. If so, center the cap between the grout joints. The slight difference in grout joint sizes will not be apparent.

If your V-cap extends below the edge of the plywood base, use a piece of scrap or your finger behind the open gap at the bottom edge to keep the grout in place.

To install a wood edge, measure pieces and miter cut the corners if desired. After the tile is set, fasten the edging to the countertop base with nails or screws. Use 6d finish nails and countersink them with a nail set. Fill the holes with colored filler that matches the wood stain. If using screws, glue plugs to hide the top of counterbored screws.

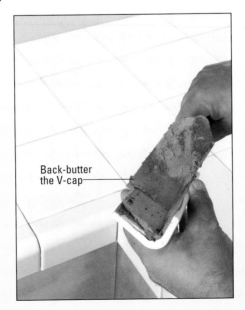

Back-butter the V-cap

6d finish nails for wood edge

D. Tiling a backsplash

1 Snap layout lines on the backsplash area to correspond to the grout lines for the tile size used. Set up the first row of tiles in a dry run, using nylon wedges to keep their top edges level. Mark the top edge on the wall and snap a level chalk line at this point, extending it beyond the end if possible.

2 Remove the dry-laid tiles and apply thinset. If the backsplash continues up to the cabinets, work in small sections. Some areas may be hard to reach and will require more time for placing the tile. Working in small sections will avoid the risk of the adhesive setting up too soon.

3 Set the bottom row of tiles using the wedges to bring it level with the line you have marked on the wall. Set the remaining tiles, cleaning the grout lines with a utility knife as you go. Use spacers if appropriate to your tile and check the lines with a straightedge. Let the mortar cure.

Installing a vanity countertop

Use the same techniques shown above to install a countertop and backsplash on a vanity. If you have removed the vanity top, build a new base and install backerboard. If tiling a vanity wall only, tile over the existing wall surface.

What if ...
Backsplash tiles are different than the countertop?

Backsplash tiles do not have to be the same as those on the countertop. You can achieve interesting decorative effects by using accent tiles or wall tiles of different dimensions.

Plan the layout carefully on paper and by laying out the tiles without mortar so that you achieve a pleasing effect with the offset grout joints.

Once you have established the layout with dry-set tiles, mark their position on the walls and snap layout lines that conform to their dimensions.

Install the tiles with the same techniques as you would other backsplash tile.

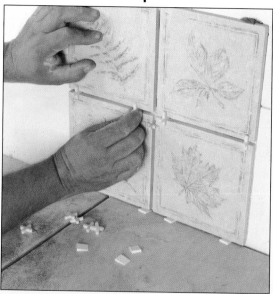

4 Remove the wedges from beneath the bottom row of tiles. Apply grout to the joints with a grout float. Do not grout the joint below the bottom row. Work the float in both directions to fill the joints. Completing an upward stroke is difficult under a cabinet. Work by pulling the float down.

5 Let the grout set until it doesn't pull out of the joint when you run a damp sponge across it lightly. Then scrape the excess grout off the tile surface. Wring out a sponge completely and smooth the joints, removing the excess from the surface. Repeat the cleaning at least one more time.

6 Using a sealant or caulk that matches the color and consistency of the grout, caulk the joint at the base of the backsplash. Apply the caulk at a consistent rate into the joint. Smooth the caulk with a wet finger.

Laying a diagonal backsplash

1 Divide the backsplash at the midpoints of both the horizontal and vertical planes. Snap perpendicular chalk lines at these points. From the intersection, measure out an equal distance on each line extending them until they intersect *(page 33)*. Draw diagonal lines connecting the intersection points.

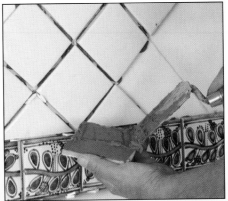

2 Using the diagonal lines as quadrants, trowel on thinset in one quadrant. Set tile within that quadrant and clean it. Then set and clean the remaining quadrants in any order. Remove any excess mortar from the joints. Let the mortar cure, then cut and install the edge tile.

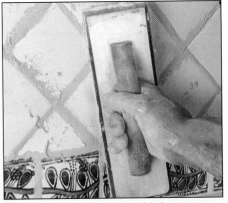

3 Force grout into the joints with the grout float, working at right angles to the joints. Let the grout set up slightly and remove the excess grout from the tile with the float. Clean the surface at least twice with a damp sponge and clean water. Scour the haze from the surface with a clean rag.

MAINTAINING & REPAIRING

Tile is one of the lowest maintenance surfaces you can install. Regular vacuuming and damp-mopping with a cleaner will keep both glazed and unglazed tiles in top condition.

Cleaning routines

Shower enclosures and tub surrounds may require special attention to remove the accumulated buildup of soap scum and water deposits and to keep mildew from forming.

Commercial products are effective cleaners, but you may find less expensive alternatives with household products you already have on hand.

Remove thin soap deposits and water spots with a vinegar solution (1 cup vinegar to 1 gallon of warm water). Weekly cleaning will keep the tile shining and prevent mildew.

Dip an old toothbrush in full strength bleach and scrub to clean the grout joints. Check colored grout in an inconspicuous place to make sure the bleach won't remove the color. Rinse everything with clear water to remove residue. Make sure the room has sufficient ventilation and be sure to wear eye protection, old clothing, and rubber gloves when using bleach or other cleaning agents. Never mix bleach with other chemicals; such mixtures can release toxic chlorine gas.

Polish metal glazed tiles with a metal polish recommended by the manufacturer, and if you have to scrub a tile surface, use a nylon scrubber. Metal scrubbers leave marks that are difficult to remove. Steel wool can scratch surfaces and leave behind metal fragments that will rust in the grout.

Assess the damage

Damaged tiles, cracked grout joints, water spots, and other forms of damage may be only superficial or may indicate more serious problems with the structure or the substrate. Try to assess the cause of the damage before making repairs.

You may be able to live with a few cracks in an old tiled surface. In fact, the cracks may add to the decorative charm. Matching an old tile pattern will likely prove difficult. Even if you can find the pattern, the tile may have developed a patina with age, and the new tiles will be more noticeable.

Water problems

If the tiles cover a surface that gets wet, however, they need attention. Water seeping through cracks may rot the substructure underneath.

Water spots may actually be the first indication of a problem in a wet area. Check the obvious sources first—damaged caulk or sealant, exposed joints at fixtures, deficient gaskets, or packing material around faucets. If the surface seems spongy, pull up a tile and check for the presence of a waterproofing membrane. If there isn't one, you'll have to take up the entire surface, repair or replace the subfloor, and reinstall a membrane, substrate, and new tile.

Simple cleaning keeps most tile in top condition. If cracks appear, look for underlying problems.

CHAPTER PREVIEW

Cleaning and sealing tiles
page 112

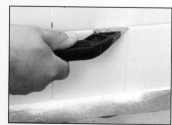

Repairing damaged surfaces
page 114

Wall tile will stand up to a lot of rough treatment. Sometimes, however, a tile that suffers a sharp blow may crack. To repair a damaged wall tile, remove the tile, scrape out the excess, and replace it with a new tile, adding mortar to the recess and the back of the replacement. When any tile needs replacing, make sure the damage was not caused by underlying problems in the substrate.

CLEANING AND SEALING TILES

Although regular cleaning will keep your tile in good condition, some surfaces, especially in kitchens and family rooms, may require stain removal.

Removing stains

When you need to remove a stain, start with the procedures outlined in the chart at right. If these solutions don't work, ask a tile supplier for a commercial stain-removal agent made for your tile. Stubborn stains will often come out with a cleaning agent mixed with baking soda, plaster of paris, or refined clay. Deodorant-free cat litter works well. Mix the ingredients into a wet paste and apply it to the stain. Tape a plastic bag over the paste and let it sit for a couple of days. Then brush off the paste.

Sealing tile

Unglazed tile almost always requires a sealer, and even presealed tile may need periodic stripping and resealing. Penetrating sealers soak into the tile bisque and preserve the natural color of the tile. Topical sealers lie on the surface of the tile and may lighten or darken the tile colors or change its sheen. Topical sealers wear off and may require reapplication yearly. When tiles look dull it is probably time to strip and reseal them.

PRESTART CHECKLIST

☐ **TIME**
About 45 minutes to vacuum and damp mop a 15×20 kitchen, 1½ hours to strip it, and about the same time to seal it

☐ **TOOLS**
Stripping: scrub brush and mop
Sealing: applicator

☐ **PREP**
Vacuum and clean surface

☐ **MATERIALS**
Stripper, sealer, bucket, rags

Stripping tiles

1 To remove old sealer, flow stripper on surface with a sponge or mop in an area (about 25 square feet) that you can clean before the liquid dries. Scrub the area with a brush or with a floor scrubbing machine. Do not let the stripper dry on surface.

2 Remove residue with a sponge or rags. Some water-based strippers allow removal with a wet-dry vacuum. Rinse with clean water and wipe dry.

REMOVING STAINS FROM TILE

Stain	Cleaner and method
Ink, coffee, blood	Start with a 3 percent hydrogen peroxide solution; if that doesn't work, try a nonbleach cleaner
Oil-based products	Mild solvent, such as charcoal lighter or mineral spirits, then household cleaner in a poultice. For dried paint, scrape with plastic (not metal) scraper.
Grease, fats	Clean with a commercial spot lifter
Rust	Use commercial rust removers; then try household cleaner
Nail polish	Remove with nail polish remover

Always rinse the stained area with clear water to remove residue.

Applying sealers

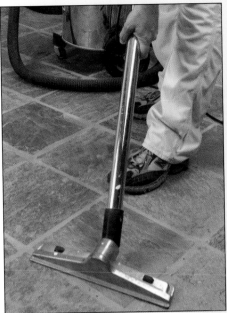

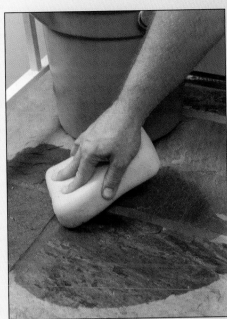

1 On newly tiled floors, wait 48 hours before sealing. On existing floors, vacuum the surface thoroughly to keep dirt and dust from becoming embedded in the new sealer.

2 With a sponge, clean the tile with a commercial tile cleaning product, following the manufacturer's directions. Rinse with clear water.

3 Apply sealer with a sponge applicator, paint pad, brush or mop, as required by the manufacturer. Do not let sealer puddle or run on walls. Some sealers cannot be overlapped. Some may require wiping with a clean rag. Allow time to dry between coats. Reapply one or two additional coats.

SAFETY FIRST
Floor care products can be toxic

Many strippers and sealers are solvent based and highly caustic. Even water-based products contain harmful chemicals. All floor-care products are potentially dangerous—observe the manufacturer's safety precautions.

Wear rubber gloves, old long-sleeve clothing, pants, and eye protection. Wear a respirator to avoid breathing toxic fumes and put a fan in the window to exhaust fumes and provide adequate ventilation. Perform tile maintenance tasks when the children are out of the house.

Working with waxes

Many unglazed tile surfaces lend themselves to waxed finishes. Some waxes contain pigments to enhance the color of the tile.

To properly renew a waxed floor, strip the old wax and wash the surface thoroughly with a mild detergent. Rinse with clear water and let it dry completely. Wax the surface in successive thin coats with the applicator recommended by the manufacturer, allowing each coat to dry and buffing in between. Repeated thin coats leave a brighter shine than one thick coat and reduce wax build-up.

A dull shine doesn't mean rewaxing. Clean the floor with a soap-free cleaner and buff with a cloth or rented buffing machine. When using a buffer, start in the middle of the floor with the brush level. Tilt the handle up or down slightly to move it from side to side. Buff across the surface. Do not push it.

REPAIRING DAMAGED SURFACES

Tile is the most durable of flooring materials, but it is not impervious to damage. Improper installation, poor adhesive bonds, and falling objects can cause it to crack or chip.

Repairing the problem begins with removing the grout and tile. Before replacing the grout and tile, however, diagnose the problem to see if you need to make a structural repair.

Cracked joints are most often caused by an improper grout mix or the absence of expansion joints. If the grout is soft and powdery, remove it and regrout. If the cracked grout is hard, remove it and fill the joint with colored caulk that matches.

Cracked tiles on a long length of floor can be caused by a faulty adhesive bond or an underlying crack. Before you remove the tiles, tap them lightly with a metal object, such as a wrench. If you hear a hollow sound, the bond is probably at fault and a thorough cleaning and new mortar will fix the problem. If the wrench "rings," the bond is probably solid; the crack may need to be isolated with a membrane.

PRESTART CHECKLIST

☐ **TIME**
About 1½ hours to remove and replace grout and tile, at least 1 day to regrout a large area

☐ **TOOLS**
Grout knife or utility knife, hammer and cold chisel, putty knife or margin trowel

☐ **SKILLS**
Breaking tile with hammer and cold chisel, driving fasteners, troweling

☐ **MATERIALS**
Thinset and grout

Removing and replacing damaged tile

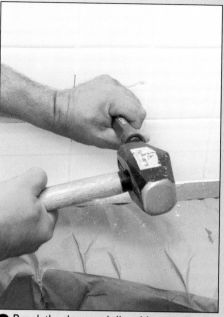

1 Score the grout around the damaged tile with a carbide grout saw or utility knife. Scoring reduces the tendency of other tiles to crack when you remove the damaged area. Protect the tub or area below with heavy paper.

2 Break the damaged tile with a small sledge and cold chisel, starting from the center of the tile and working to the edges.

Adding a towel bar to a tile wall

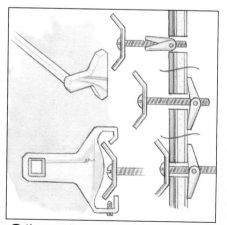

1 Mark the location of the accessory on the wall, level and centered on the studs if possible. Nick the glaze with a sharp awl and hammer at the mark. Use a masonry drill bit to drill through the tile and anchor the hangers to the studs with wood screws.

2 If you can't center the accessory on the studs, drill through the tile and the wall. Insert a toggle bolt screw into the hanger and refasten the toggles. Push the toggles through the hole until they expand. Tighten the screw until the fixture is secure.

3 Remove the broken pieces, prying them out with a putty knife or margin trowel if necessary. Scrape off the old adhesive from the wall.

4 Back-butter the new tile with a sufficiently thick coat of mortar. If possible, use the same adhesive or mortar used on the old tile. Use thinset if you don't know what mortar was originally used.

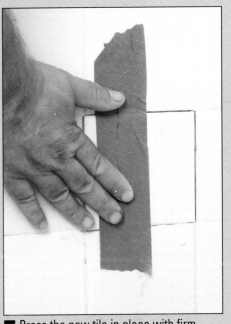

5 Press the new tile in place with firm pressure. Make sure it's level with the rest of the surface. Remove the tile and adjust the layer of mortar if necessary. Center the tile in the recess. Nails or spacers will help keep it aligned. Tape the tile until the mortar cures, then apply grout.

Repairing tile on a cracked slab

1 Remove grout from the joints along the entire length of the crack, including at least one tile beyond those damaged. Following the manufacturer's directions apply adhesive and isolation membrane.

2 Trowel thinset into the recess and back-butter each tile. Replace the tiles and level them. Grout and clean when the mortar is dry.

APPLY GROUT
Regrouting a small area

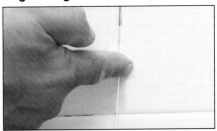

When regrouting a small area or a single replacement tile, take out the old grout with a utility knife or grout knife. Unless you are replacing the grout on the entire area, try to match the color of the existing grout. Mix a small batch and let it dry; then compare it with the grout already on the tiles.

   If grouting a large area, apply the grout with a float. On a small area or a single tile, use your finger to press the grout into the joint. Shape the grout with a wet sponge.

GLOSSARY

Actual dimensions: The actual size of a tile. as measured with a tape or ruler. *See nominal dimension.*

Back-butter: To apply mortar or adhesive to the rear face of a tile before setting it.

Backerboard: Any of several cement or gypsum-based sheets used as substrate for setting tile. *See cement board.*

Backsplash: Surface that abuts or is attached to the rear of a countertop along its entire length, typically 3 to 4 inches high.

Beater block: Manufactured or home-made tool covered with soft surface. Used to set tiles level on surface.

Bisque: The clay-and-liquid mixture that forms the body of the tile.

Bond strength: The measure of an adhesive's ability to resist separating from tile and setting bed when cured.

Brick veneer: Any of several products in various thicknesses made of clay or other materials and additives whose appearance resembles brick.

Building codes: Ordinances established by local communities to govern quality and construction methods used in building a home or other structure.

Bullnose tiles: Flat tile with at least one rounded edge. Used to trim the edges of a tiled installation. Also called caps.

Butt joint: A joint formed when two surfaces meet exactly on their edges, ends or faces.

Casing: Wood or other material around the perimeter of a door, window, or other opening in a wall.

Caulk: Any of several compounds used to seal surface gaps or joints. Applied in semi-liquid form from tubes or a caulking gun, it dries to flexible bead that keeps out liquids. Available in a wide range of colors and in sanded or unsanded mixtures.

Cement board: A type of backerboard made from a cement base and coated or impregnated with fiberglass mesh.

Cement-bodied tile: Tile whose bisque is formed of mortar as opposed to clay.

Ceramic tile: A type of tile composed of refined clay usually mixed with additives and water and hardened by firing in a kiln to a minimum of 1800°F. Can be glazed or unglazed.

Control joint: An intentional gap cut or formed in a concrete surface to control where the surface cracks.

Cove base: Describes a type of floor trim tile whose base is curved inward.

Down angle: A trim tile with two rounded edges used to finish off an outside corner.

Drywall: A gypsum-based sheet product covered on both sides with paper and used to finish interior wall surfaces.

Expansion joint: An intended space or gap built into materials subject to cracking. Allows materials to expand and contract with temperature changes without damage to the remainder of the surface.

Extruded: Describes the process of shaping a tile by pressing it into a die.

Field tiles: Flat tiles with unrounded edges used within the edges of a tiled installation.

Float: A flat, rectangular wood or metal hand tool used for smoothing mortared surfaces

Flush: Having the same surface or plane as an adjoining surface.

Glaze: A hard, most often colored layer of lead silicates and other materials fired to the surface of a tile. Used to protect and decorate the tile surface.

Granite: A naturally occurring stone composed of quartz and other minerals. Generally found in reds or browns.

Greenboard: A moisture-resistant drywall product made for wet installations, such as baths and showers. Greenboard is not waterproof.

Grout: A mortar mix used to fill the joints between set tiles. Available in a wide range of colors and in sanded or unsanded mixtures.

Grout float: A float with a soft rubber surface used to press grout into tile joints.

Hang: Describes the ability of an adhesive to hold a tile on a vertical surface while the adhesive is still wet.

Impervious tile: Tiles whose density resists completely the absorption of liquids. Generally used in hospitals, restaurants, and other commercial locations.

Inside corner: The plane on which walls or other surfaces form an internal angle.

Isolation membrane: A flexible sheet or liquid product applied to subsurface of a tile installation to allow cracks to expand under the tile without telegraphing into the surface.

Jamb: The surface of wood or other material on the immediate side or top and bottom of a door or window frame.

Joint compound: A plaster-like product used with paper or fiberglass mesh tape to conceal joints between drywall panels.

Layout lines: Chalklines snapped to guide the placement of tile.

Level: Having all surfaces exactly on the same plane. Also describes a hand tool used to determine level.

Marble: A naturally occurring hard variation of limestone marked with varied color and vein patterns.

Masonry cement: A powdered mixture of portland cement and hydrated lime used for preparing mortar. Used to bind sand or other aggregate materials together.

Mexican paver: A handmade tile, generally low fired or sundried and unglazed, characterized by blemishes, imperfections and irregular edges.

Mortar: Any mixture of masonry cement, sand, water, and other additives. Also describes the action of applying mortar to surfaces or joints.

Mosaic tile: Any tile less than 2 inches, generally vitreous and made in squares or hexagons. Generally mounted on sheets or joined with adhesive strips.

Nippers: *See tile nippers.*

Nominal dimensions: The stated size of a tile, representing the ratio of one side to the other and usually including the width of its normal grout joint. Not necessarily the actual dimensions of the material. *See actual dimensions.*

Nonvitreous tile: Low density tile whose pores absorb liquids readily. Generally used indoors in dry locations.

Organic mastic: One of several petroleum or latex-based adhesives for setting tiles. Exhibits less strength, flexibility, and resistance to water than thinset adhesives.

Outside corner: The plane on which walls or other surfaces form an angle.

Particleboard: A sheet product made from compressed wood chips and glue. Not as durable and exhibits less screw-holding power than plywood of similar thicknesses.

Pavers: Any of several vitreous clay, shale, porcelain, or cement-bodied floor tiles, from ½- to 2-inches thick and unglazed.

Plumb: A surface that lies on a true vertical plane.

Plumb bob: A weight, generally pointed, suspended on a line or string, used to determine is a surface is truly vertical or plumb.

Quarry tile: Unglazed, vitreous or semi-vitreous tiles, usually ¼- to ½-inch thick, most often used on floors.

Rod saw: A tungsten-carbide blade with a rounded surface set in a standard hacksaw frame and used for cutting curves in tile.

Sealer: Any of several topical or penetrating products used as a protective coating on grout and unglazed tile surfaces.

Semi-vitreous tile: Tile of moderate density which exhibits only a partial resistance to water and other liquids.

Slate: A naturally occurring stone composed of compressed shale deposits, generally rough surfaced and grey or black.

Snap cutter: A bench-mounted tool consisting of a carbide scribing wheel and a pressure plate that cut straight cuts in tile by snapping it along a scribed line.

Spacers: Small plastic pieces, usually x-shaped, used to ensure consistent grout-joint width between tiles.

Square: Surfaces exactly perpendicular or at 90-degrees to another. Also describes a hand tool used to determine square.

Stone tile: Naturally occurring materials that are cut from quarries and sliced or hand split into thin sections for use as tile. Generally marble, granite, flagstone, and slate.

Straightedge: A length of metal or wood with a perfectly straight surface. Used to mark a straight line on material or to determine if edges or surfaces are on the same plane.

Subfloor: A layer of wood sheet material, generally plywood, used to provide a stable foundation for other flooring materials.

Substrate: Any of several layers, including the subfloor, beneath a tile surface.

Taping: Describes the process of applying paper or mesh tape to drywall joints in preparation for application of joint compound.

Thin-set mortar: Generic term used to describe a wide range of mortar-based tile adhesives.

Tile nippers: A hand tool similar to a pliers but with levered jaws of hardened steel. Used for cutting small notches and curves in tile.

Toenail: Act of driving a nail at an angle to a surface when joining two pieces attached on dissimilar planes.

Trim tile: Tiles with at least one rounded or otherwise configured edge, used at corners or to define the edges of an installation. Common examples are cove trim, bullnose, V-cap, quarter-round, inside corners, and outside corners.

Trowel: Any of several flat and rectangular or pointed metal hand tools used for applying and smoothing adhesives and mortars.

Up angle: Describes a trim tile with one rounded edge used to finish an inside corner.

V-cap: V-shaped trim, often with a rounded upper corner used to edge countertops.

Vitreous tile: An extremely dense ceramic tile with a high resistance to water absorption. Used indoors or outdoors, in wet or dry locations.

Waterproofing membrane: Any of several synthetic sheet materials used with or without adhesives to make a surface waterproof. Polyethylene and 15-lb. felt paper are common examples.

Wet saw: A high-speed power saw equipped with a water-cooled carbide blade used for cutting straight cuts in tile.

INDEX

METRIC CONVERSIONS

U.S. Units to Metric Equivalents			Metric Units to U.S. Equivalents		
To convert from	Multiply by	To get	To convert from	Multiply by	To get
Inches	25.4	Millimeters	Millimeters	0.0394	Inches
Inches	2.54	Centimeters	Centimeters	0.3937	Inches
Feet	30.48	Centimeters	Centimeters	0.0328	Feet
Feet	0.3048	Meters	Meters	3.2808	Feet
Yards	0.9144	Meters	Meters	1.0936	Yards
Square inches	6.4516	Square centimeters	Square centimeters	0.1550	Square inches
Square feet	0.0929	Square meters	Square meters	10.764	Square feet
Square yards	0.8361	Square meters	Square meters	1.1960	Square yards
Acres	0.4047	Hectares	Hectares	2.4711	Acres
Cubic inches	16.387	Cubic centimeters	Cubic centimeters	0.0610	Cubic inches
Cubic feet	0.0283	Cubic meters	Cubic meters	35.315	Cubic feet
Cubic feet	28.316	Liters	Liters	0.0353	Cubic feet
Cubic yards	0.7646	Cubic meters	Cubic meters	1.308	Cubic yards
Cubic yards	764.55	Liters	Liters	0.0013	Cubic yards

To convert from degrees Fahrenheit (F) to degrees Celsius (C), first subtract 32, then multiply by ⅝.

To convert from degrees Celsius to degrees Fahrenheit, multiply by ⅝, then add 32.